Classroom Adventures

Center-Based
Themes For Early Childhood

Written by
Karen V. Jones

Edited by
Ada Goren

Illustrated by
Pam Crane, Teresa R. Davidson,
Sheila Krill, Theresa Lewis,
Kimberly Richard,
Rebecca Saunders

D1530426

Cover designed by
Kimberly Richard

©1999 by THE EDUCATION CENTER, INC.
All rights reserved.
ISBN# 1-56234-313-0

Manufactured in the United States
10 9 8 7 6 5 4 3 2 1

Table Of Contents

Introduction

What's the key to a young child's academic success? It's an immersion into science, language, and math all wrapped up in a wonderful package called *play!* Play is a child's work. It's the means by which a child makes discoveries and builds knowledge of the world around him. It's a safe and natural way for him to try out new roles, experiment with objects, utilize his senses, and express his creativity. Where does the teacher fit into all this? He or she is a facilitator, readying the environment, providing materials, and opening up possibilities for new explorations along the way.

With that theory in mind, this book strives to provide you with a myriad of developmentally appropriate ideas that have been field-tested by hundreds of inquisitive youngsters just like the ones you teach! Each unit in *Classroom Adventures* is a map that will take your class on a journey without leaving your school. You'll find ideas for your favorite centers that will help you transform your classroom into an exciting environment just full of possibilities for learning! There's enough creative fuel stored in these pages to take you from coast to coast or just around the corner. All it takes is a little planning and a whole lot of imagination!

And while your students are exploring, they'll be developing important skills, which you'll see listed next to each and every center idea. You'll also find activities to get parents involved and an open reproducible at the end of each unit, so you can share with them the highlights of your trips.

So pick a destination and pack your bags. And remember that the most important thing—the thing that will have children bounding into your room each day with wide smiles, the thing that will motivate you to get to school early, stay late, or make that extra trip to the discount store, the thing that everyone loves—is to have FUN!

Packing Your Bags

There are a few basics that you'll want to bring along regardless of the classroom adventure you choose. The following materials are standard in most units, so having them packed and ready to go will give you more time to enjoy the journey.

Collage Collectibles

Recycling everything but the kitchen sink *must* be a prerequisite to great teaching! Create categories of collage materials that complement each other and provide a variety of interest in texture and color. You may need to prepare small pieces of some materials for easy handling and cutting, but allow plenty of room for self-expression and exploration.

Begin with:

colored cellophane cut into strips or squares; assorted tissue paper; crepe paper streamers; curling ribbon; Mylar® scraps; aluminum foil; shredded or crinkled gift packaging; wrapping paper; sequins; buttons; dyed macaroni; foil confetti; Styrofoam® peanuts; shredded computer paper; Easter grass; popcorn kernels; dried beans; birdseed; fabric scraps; wallpaper squares; bits of yarn, lace, and rickrack; chenille stems ...*and add anything else you can find!*

"Plue"

This is a mixture of one part white school paste and one part white school glue. It can be tinted any color with a touch of tempera. Stir until it almost resembles frosting. It will adhere nearly anything to any surface, dry hard, and wash off in a jiffy. It also s-t-r-e-t-c-h-e-s your glue budget and keeps indefinitely in the fridge.

Sensory-Table Utensils

Rarely filled with only sand or water, the sensory tables in each unit provide experiences rich with science, math, and language...not to mention socialization! Having some of the following utensils on hand will allow you to simplify or challenge each child according to her developmental ability.

Try these kitchen utensils:

slotted spoons; ladles; spatulas; wooden spoons; ice-cream scoops; pasta forks; potato mashers; tongs; colanders; measuring cups; funnels; strainers; turkey basters; mixing bowls; muffin tins; cake pans
...*and keep your eye out for other great tools to use!*

ADMIT ONE

Glittery Stuff

Whether it's in artwork, play dough, or water tables, a pinch of glitter makes the ordinary extraordinary! To make glitter go twice as far, add one part table salt to one part glitter. Mix a variety of colors ahead of time and store them in plastic bags or airtight containers. Foil confetti, available in the party section of craft and toy stores, is a must-have on your supply list. It's fun to use, easy to clean up, and costs just a penny a pinch!

Tempera Paint

Premix one part liquid dish detergent into two parts tempera paint to make cleanup easier. Store the paint in gallon jugs or pour it back into detergent bottles. You'll have a rainbow at your fingertips!

Homemade "Watery-colors"

Stir a few drops of food coloring into a bowl of water. Add a splash of vinegar. Make a variety of colors and store them in airtight containers. This will keep indefinitely!

Sugar Chalk

This is like paint on a stick! Add one part sugar to four parts very hot water and drop in sticks of colored sidewalk chalk. Wait for about five minutes or until all the fizzing stops. Pull the chalk out of the sugar water and draw with it immediately. Or let the chalk dry and then store it in a plastic bag. When you're ready to use it, dunk it into plain water first; then draw. Note: Do _not_ use this on chalkboards. Use on paper only.

Monoprints

When you want children to paint BIG and w-i-d-e on the surfaces of tables, trays, or easels instead of directly on paper, use this technique to send a piece of artwork home. Simply press a piece of paper on part of the design, rub, and then peel it off. Ta da!

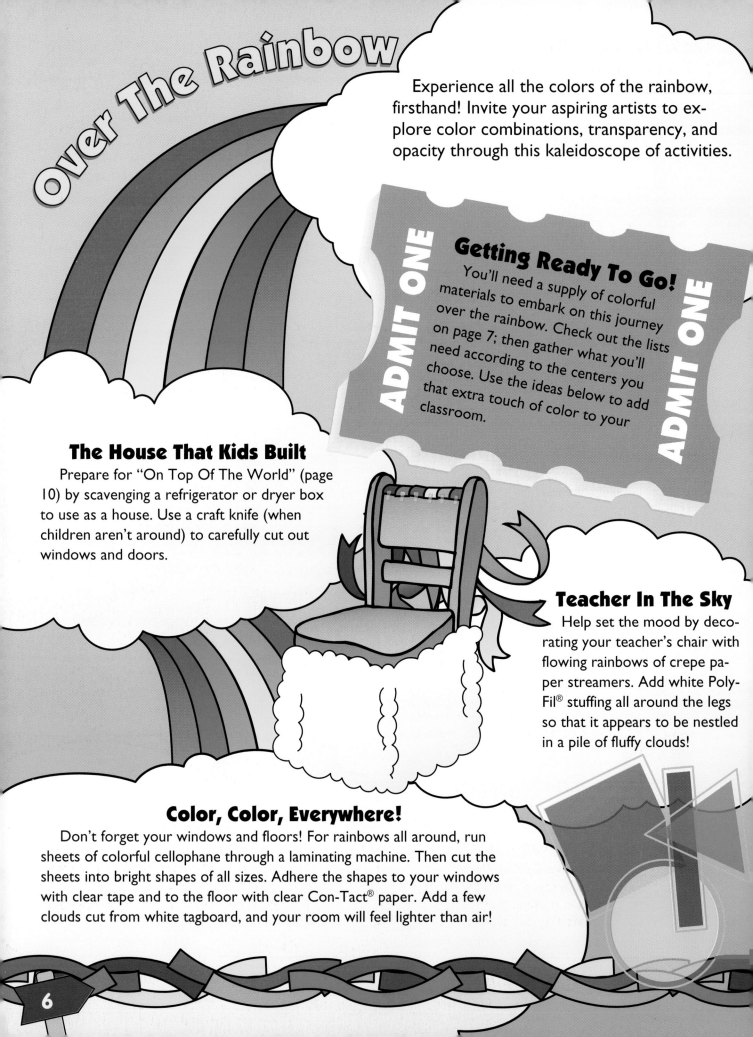

Over The Rainbow

Experience all the colors of the rainbow, firsthand! Invite your aspiring artists to explore color combinations, transparency, and opacity through this kaleidoscope of activities.

ADMIT ONE

Getting Ready To Go!

You'll need a supply of colorful materials to embark on this journey over the rainbow. Check out the lists on page 7; then gather what you'll need according to the centers you choose. Use the ideas below to add that extra touch of color to your classroom.

ADMIT ONE

The House That Kids Built

Prepare for "On Top Of The World" (page 10) by scavenging a refrigerator or dryer box to use as a house. Use a craft knife (when children aren't around) to carefully cut out windows and doors.

Teacher In The Sky

Help set the mood by decorating your teacher's chair with flowing rainbows of crepe paper streamers. Add white Poly-Fil® stuffing all around the legs so that it appears to be nestled in a pile of fluffy clouds!

Color, Color, Everywhere!

Don't forget your windows and floors! For rainbows all around, run sheets of colorful cellophane through a laminating machine. Then cut the sheets into bright shapes of all sizes. Adhere the shapes to your windows with clear tape and to the floor with clear Con-Tact® paper. Add a few clouds cut from white tagboard, and your room will feel lighter than air!

Color Collectibles

Choose from the center ideas on pages 8–13. Here's a handy list of the supplies you'll need to prepare each one.

Art Area

Create-A-Color Collages: red, yellow, and blue cellophane; clear Con-Tact® covering; crepe paper (optional); scissors
Now You See It…: small white paper plates, colored tissue paper shapes, water in saltshakers
Collaborative Creations: red, yellow, and blue tempera paint; trays; small paint rollers; large pieces of paper or tagboard
Rainbows All Around: record player, thin paper plates, markers

Reading Center

Fluff 'n' Stuff: small plastic pool, white Poly-Fil® stuffing, pillows

Writing Center

The End Of The Rainbow: marker, tagboard, watercolors or crayons
Colorful Stories: cloud-shaped white paper, crayons

Dramatic-Play Center

It's Dinnertime!: colored cellophane strips, kitchen tongs, colanders, large mixing bowls, yellow or red tablecloth

Sensory Tables And Tubs

Rainbows In A Tub: colored cellophane strips, pasta forks
A Sea Of Color: colored cellophane squares, slotted spoons, large plastic or metal bowls
Cloud Clusters…Boredom Busters!: white Styrofoam® packing peanuts, dish detergent, large plastic spoons
Around In A Circle: colored masking tape, metal bowls, rubber spatulas

Block Area

On Top Of The World: box house, scrap paper or art tissue squares, glue sticks, white Poly-Fil® stuffing

Science Center

Rainbows In A Bottle: plastic soft drink bottles (with caps), colored cellophane shapes or transparent colored counting chips, hot glue
Sprinkle…Squish…Sculpt!: white play dough, powdered tempera paints in saltshakers

Art Area

Cognitive skills
Fine-motor skills
Color and shape discrimination
Sequencing
Visual expression

Create-A-Color Collages

Transform cellophane strips into colorful creations with the help of some clear Con-Tact® paper. Supply red, yellow, and blue cellophane strips; scissors; and a piece of Con-Tact® paper for each child. You might provide colored crepe paper as well. Help each artist place her Con-Tact® paper sticky side up. Then demonstrate how to place the cellophane strips on the sticky paper—no glue required!

Ask the children to see if they can invent some *new* colors using their strips. You'll want to hang the finished projects in your windows for a room that dances with rainbows!

Now You See It...

Invite children to make rainbows "melt" into the clouds. Have a child sprinkle shredded or cut tissue paper shapes onto a small white paper plate, then moisten the tissue pieces with "rain" from salt-shakers filled with water. The colors from the tissue paper will transfer onto the plate, leaving behind a beautiful print.

Charody and Benjamin

Collaborative Creations

When it comes to blending paint, two artists are better than one! Gather red, yellow, and blue tempera paint; then put a small amount of each on separate trays. Add small rollers to the paint and provide a big piece of paper or tagboard. Invite a pair of children to paint, and it won't be long before rainbows of every color appear! Be sure to put both names on the masterpiece and display it for all to see!

Rainbows All Around

Jazz up your art area by plugging in your record player and letting children color with markers on paper-plate "records." They'll be amazed to see the designs that appear! Encourage children to try to hold more than one marker at a time or to color at the same time as a friend.
(Tip: You'll want to have lots of plates on hand for this station!)

Reading Center

Vocabulary development
Attention span
Receptive and expressive language skills
Colors and color words

Fluff 'n' Stuff

For a sensation that's out of this world, fill a plastic pool with fluffy, white Poly-Fil® stuffing. Throw in a couple of soft pillows and some favorite books to create the mood of a reading center high in the sky, in the land of rainbows. This feels so good—even teachers will be tempted to hop in!

Colorful Story Selections

Brighten up your storytime (and your reading center shelves) with these book choices.

Cat's Colors
By Jane Cabrera
Dial Books For Young Readers

Mouse Paint
By Ellen Stoll Walsh
Voyager Picture Books

My Crayons Talk
By Patricia Hubbard
Henry Holt And Company, Inc.

Chuck Murphy's Color Surprises: A Pop-Up Book
By Chuck Murphy
Little Simon

Who Said Red?
By Mary Serfozo
Aladdin Paperbacks

Of Colors And Things
By Tana Hoban
Mulberry Books

Eye Spy Colors
By Debbie MacKinnon
Charlesbridge Publishing

Dramatic-Play Center

Creative thinking
Verbal skills
Socialization

It's Dinnertime!

Add a splash of color to your menu with strips of colored cellophane. Kitchen tongs, colanders, and large mixing bowls are perfect partners for any chef preparing a colorful creation. A bright yellow or red tablecloth will add a little sunshine to your kitchen!

Block Area

Fine-motor skills
Gross-motor skills
Cognitive skills
Counting
Patterning
Socialization

On Top Of The World

What would it feel like to actually live on a rainbow or in the clouds? Invite your children to explore that question with a make-believe house in the clouds. Bring out the box you prepared in "The House That Kids Built" (page 6). Provide glue sticks and scrap paper or art tissue squares. Encourage your children to create a "dream home" to add to your block area. Provide white Poly-Fil® stuffing to serve as clouds; then let the creative dramatics begin. Let's see…how about a fence over here and a long brick driveway around the back?

Sensory Tables And Tubs

Fine-motor skills
Sensory discrimination
Color and shape recognition
Socialization

Rainbows In A Tub

Fill a tub with colorful cellophane strips and some pasta forks. Children will be fascinated with the color and sound of so many rainbows.

Cloud Clusters...Boredom Busters!

Pour white Styrofoam® packing peanuts into a tub or baby pool; then add lots of dish detergent and a little water to make the peanuts stick together. Provide big plastic spoons. The more the children stir, the "globbier" the clouds get! This station can last for a week at a time. Simply add clean water each morning and stir. To save your clouds for another day, rinse the packing peanuts thoroughly. Then let them air-dry and pack them in a box.

A Sea Of Color

Toss a couple of handfuls of colored cellophane squares in a tub and add water. All you need now are some slotted spoons and big plastic or metal bowls to float on top.

Around In A Circle

Stick strips of colored masking tape inside metal bowls in a spiral "spinning top" pattern. Then float the bowls in a pool or tub of water. Add rubber spatulas for getting the spinning started. Children will be dizzy with wonder when they see themselves in swirling rainbows!

Writing Center

Creative language and thought processing
Word association
Writing
Socialization

I see a big garden with flowers in all the colors. Jenna

On the other end of the rainbow is a big lake with purple water. I'm going in a boat. Phillip

The End Of The Rainbow

What's *really* at the end of the rainbow? Create a class story about the surprising things your children would find if they could slide down the other side of a rainbow! Use a permanent marker to write children's ideas on tagboard; then invite them to use watercolors or crayons to illustrate their tale. This story could grow all week....

Colorful Stories

Encourage children to use *lots* of colors as they create their own rainbow stories on cloud-shaped pages. Cut white construction paper into the shape of big clouds. And be sure to provide the big 64-count box of crayons!

Rainbows In A Bottle

Gather a collection of clear plastic soft drink bottles (any size from 16-ounce to three-liter). Fill each bottle with water to the rim; then add colored cellophane shapes or transparent colored counting chips (found in the math section of parent-teacher stores). Seal each cap tightly, adding a bit of hot glue for protection against leaks. Children of all ages love to see the rainbows on the floor when they roll, stack, and build with these bottles.

Sprinkle...Squish...Sculpt!

Let's grow Rainbow Dough! Children will love exploring color as they create their own spectrum of colored play dough. Provide several colors of powdered tempera paint in saltshakers. Invite children to sprinkle and shake powdered paint onto balls of white play dough, then squish the color in! A little red, a little yellow...hey! Look!

Tips For An Extended Stay

Once your centers are bursting with color, extend your theme to include a group project, outdoor fun, and family ties.

All Together Now

If your youngsters enjoy making "Create-A-Color Collages" (page 8), then invite them to collaborate on a group masterpiece. Cut a rectangle from the center of a colorful sheet of poster board to create a frame. Adhere clear Con-Tact® paper to one side; then lay the frame with the Con-Tact® paper sticky side up on a large table. Provide a big bowl of cellophane strips and squares, curling ribbon pieces, and crepe paper streamers. Encourage the children to add rainbows of color as they wish. Display the finished project in a sunny window for everyone to enjoy.

Out 'n' About

Head outdoors on a sunny day and have a Rainbow Romp! Prepare a handful of color by twisting a pipe cleaner around a bunch of colored cellophane strips (as you would to make a pom-pom). Give each child two of these rainbow shakers. Then bring the boom box outside and make sure everyone has plenty of room to wiggle and jiggle!

Family Focus

Treat parents to an afternoon of rainbows! In advance, have your students help you prepare several batches of gelatin—each a different color. Set out clear plastic cups, plastic spoons, and cans of squirtable whipped cream. Invite each child and parent to scoop some gelatin (in her choice of colors) into a cup and then top this edible rainbow with a whipped-cream "cloud"! While everyone is eating, have children take turns sharing the stories they wrote about being over the rainbow (see page 12).

Highlights Of Our Trip
Over The Rainbow

What's over the rainbow? We know—and it's better than gold! Here's some of the fun we had exploring color, light, and movement.

Fun In Fairy-Tale Land

With a wink of your eye and some good old-fashioned stardust, you can turn your classroom into a place where dreams really *do* come true! Children delight in fun and fantasy as they explore materials that shimmer and shine…and discover what it feels like to be king or queen for the day!

Getting Ready To Go!

Prepare for this journey to the magical land of make-believe by gathering the supplies you need from the lists on page 17 (depending on your choice of centers). Then create—perhaps with the help of your students—the props described below. Now, let's make believe….

Save That Box!

Refrigerator and dryer boxes can't be beat when you need a castle that's almost as big as life! Using a utility knife, carefully cut out windows and doors. Add bulletin-board borders around the edges for a warm touch. Invite children to paint the boxes with tempera paint or to add scraps of foil and shiny gift wrap for castles that really shine!

Royal Garb

Old bathrobes become fancy capes with the help of your trusty glue gun, fake fur pieces, sequins, shiny buttons, and rick-rack. Dress-up shoes transform with a coat of school glue and a pinch of glitter. And simple, everyday hats take on a whole new character when feathers, felt, costume jewelry, and sequins are added. Be daring!

Ballroom Dancing, Anyone?

To create the authentic look of royal ballroom floors, glue black construction-paper squares onto large sheets of white tagboard in a checkerboard pattern. Laminate the finished mats. Use these washable mats at each station in your room.

Fairy-Tale Fun Stuff

Choose from the center ideas on pages 18–23. Here's a handy list of the supplies you'll need to prepare each one.

Art Area

Magical Wands: unsharpened pencils, small Styrofoam® plates, collage items, "plue"

One-Size-Fits-All Royal Headdress: tagboard strips, craft items, "plue," scissors, construction paper

Swirl, Scrub, 'n' Shine: clear dish detergent, glitter, dish mops, aluminum foil, squeegee

Royal Jewels: chenille stems, "stringable" craft items

Reading Center

Who Sits On The Throne?: fake fur, fancy fabric pieces, beaded jewelry

Writing Center

King Or Queen For A Day: paper, crayons

Castle Compositions: construction paper cut into castle shapes, crayons or washable markers

Dramatic-Play Center

Cookin' Up A Feast!: large cooking pans, utensils, pot holders, apron

Setting The Table: colorful sheets or fabric pieces, aluminum pie plates, silverware, cloth napkins, unbreakable candlesticks

Dress-Ups: fancy dress-up clothes

Music And Movement

Care To Dance?: recordings of classical music, large squares of silky fabric

Sensory Tables And Tubs

In The King's Kitchen: shaving cream, food coloring, slotted spoons, plastic bowls

Sweet Dreams: sequins, utensils, clear plastic or silver bowls

Yippee! It's A Treasure Chest!: strands of plastic, beaded, Christmas-tree garland; clear dish detergent; tongs

Glitter Dough: glitter or foil confetti, teacher-made play dough

Science Center

Bubble Wishes: bubble solution and wands, food coloring, large sheets of tagboard, markers

Block Area

Castles Under Construction: aluminum foil, wooden blocks

The Magic Moat: sand/water table, toy horses, dinosaurs, plastic blocks

Art Area

Fine-motor skills
Hand-eye coordination
Cognitive skills
Visual expression
Creativity

Magical Wands

Simply insert unsharpened pencils into Styrofoam® plates (as shown). Set out tinted "plue" (see page 4) and a tray of collage materials, and children will have the beginnings of their own magical wands!

One-Size-Fits-All Royal Headdress

Having a splendid shiny crown is a *must* for every king and queen! Cut a class supply of 3" x 20" tagboard strips. Bring out your hidden treasure chest of foil confetti, plastic beads, and sequins, as well as a supply of "plue" (see page 4); then let the crowning ceremony begin! Invite children to cut points for their crowns from construction paper, if they like. When the glue has dried, staple each crown to fit its maker's head.

Swirl, Scrub, 'n' Shine

Turn your easel into something to *really* sparkle about! Devise a special "painting potion" by adding glitter to clear dish detergent. Instead of using brushes to apply this glittery stuff, take a trip to the cleaning section of most grocery stores, and you'll find a variety of dish mops that can be transformed into terrific "painting wands." Instead of painting on paper, cover the easel with aluminum foil and encourage children to swirl, scrub, and shine to their heart's content. Then squeegee off the suds and start all over again!

If desired, press a clean sheet of paper onto the glittery design and rub. Voilà! You have a monoprint to send home.

Royal Jewels

Preschoolers can easily concoct their very own "jeweled" bracelets by stringing dyed macaroni, buttons, cut straws, plastic beads, jingle bells, and bits of colorful netting through plain or glittery chenille stems. Just twist and tuck the ends to form a jangly, dangly bangle!

Receptive and expressive language skills
Vocabulary development
Attention span

Who Sits On The Throne?

You do, of course! Don't be shy…it's your turn to be queen for the day, too! Add a flair to your teacher's chair with a few of your favorite bangles and beads! Don't forget the fake fur, silks, and other finery that will transform your chair into a royal throne for storytime. And what a fine place to enjoy a good book from the reading center! (Hint: This is a great prop for photos of all your knights, kings, princesses, and queens throughout the unit, too!)

Stories Fit For A King Or Queen

Of course, you'll want to share several favorite fairy tales with your little ones. Then read aloud these fun, interactive stories. Place these books in your reading center for youngsters to enjoy throughout your fairy-tale unit.

Whose Tale Is This?
By Charles Reasoner
Price Stern Sloan, Inc.

Each Peach, Pear, Plum
By Janet and Allan Ahlberg
Puffin Books

Once Upon A Time
By John Prater
Candlewick Press

Dramatic-Play Center

Creative thinking
Verbal skills
Measurement skills
Sorting
Sequencing
Socialization

Cookin' Up A Feast!

Bring out the bundt pans, turkey roasters, Dutch ovens, and casserole dishes in order to feed the hungry crowd at the palace. Add a few interesting utensils, pot holders, and a chef's apron for authenticity. (A tip from the chief cook: Recycled Easter grass makes a lovely dish and goes an awfully long way....)

Setting The Table

A royal dining room would never be complete without fine table linens and silver! Create a formal tablecloth with colorful old sheets or fabric pieces. Add aluminum pie plates, real silverware settings, cloth napkins, and an elegant pair of unbreakable candlesticks.

Dress-Ups

Provide an old trunk or suitcase full of dress-up clothes for your young royals. In addition to any "Royal Garb" you may have made (see page 16), toss in tutus, scarves, fancy gloves, hats, bow ties, etc. Some moms may still have their old prom dresses or bridesmaids' gowns that could easily be cut down for preschool playtime. Couldn't hurt to ask!

Fine-motor skills
Color and shape discrimination
Measurement skills
Counting
Sorting
Socialization

In The King's Kitchen

Your palace chefs can whip up a feast fit for a king in this sensory center. Float shaving cream clouds in a tub of water tinted with food coloring. Include slotted kitchen spoons and some plastic bowls. You may want to position this away from your dramatic-play center...or you'll *really* have a smorgasbord!

Sweet Dreams

Fill your sensory table with water and a fistful of sparkling sequins. This mesmerizing interaction takes children to the land of daydreams in a flash! Add rubber spatulas or plastic slotted spoons, as well as clear plastic or silver bowls to float on top.

Glitter Dough

Simply add glitter or foil confetti to your favorite homemade play dough recipe, omitting the food coloring. This feels the same as colored play dough, but has an unusual sparkle and shine. You may want to make this a surprise addition to your dramatic-play area. Be sure to add rolling pins and other fancy utensils!

Yippee! It's A Treasure Chest!

Fill a tub, pool, or sensory table with colorful strands of plastic, beaded Christmas-tree garland (left on the string). Add enough clear dish detergent to make the beads slippery. Add a little water, if needed. Kitchen tongs are *lots* of fun at this station!

Music And Movement

Auditory skills
Gross-motor skills
Creative thinking
Socialization

Care To Dance?

Create a royal ambiance by playing lively classical music suited for a masquerade ball. Invite children to try out their "magical wands" (page 18) as they move and sway across the ballroom floor. Have on hand a supply of large silky fabric squares that children can transform into banners, cloaks, fancy skirts, or gowns. Mardi Gras masks would be the perfect touch!

Writing Center

Creative language and thought processing
Word association
Writing skills
Socialization

King Or Queen For A Day

Have a child dictate what it would be like if he or she were king or queen for a day. Would it rain marshmallows? Would all the moms and dads have to play hide-and-seek in the castle instead of going to work? Would every boy and girl in the whole wide world come to his or her spend-the-night party? Be sure to display these short stories for all to see.

There once wuz a fair princes who lived in a beutiful castle.

Cory

Castle Compositions

Children create the most fantastic fairy tales of all! Encourage them to design their own stories on castle-shaped sheets of quality construction paper (the kind that will last for years in a mom's special scrapbook). Simply trim sheets of paper to resemble a castle shape (as shown); then set out crayons or washable markers and let your royal scribes begin.

I wished for ice cream! Katie

I wished for a cat! J.T.

I wished for us to keep playing bubbles. Eva

Science Center

Gross-motor skills
Color and shape discrimination
Exploration of cause and effect
Verbal skills

Bubble Wishes

Designate a corner of your room as the Bubble Wish center. Fill a baby pool or shallow tub halfway with your favorite bubble solution that's been tinted with a touch of food coloring. Tuck large pieces of tagboard around the pool to "catch" the wishes. Add two or three bubble wands and watch children's wishes come to life! When the bubbles have popped and the imprints have dried on the tagboard, invite children to dictate what some of their wishes were. Use colorful markers to write the wishes on and around the bubble prints. Then display this collaborative Bubble Wish mural in your classroom.

Block Area

Gross-motor skills
Counting
Sorting
Sequencing
Size and weight discrimination
Socialization

Castles Under Construction

A favorite with all castle builders, the block area is an instant hit when some of the blocks are silver and shiny. Have your young builders help you cover some blocks with foil. You'll want to take pictures of the elaborate, one-of-a-kind kingdoms your students dream up!

The Magic Moat

Try putting your sand and water table near the block area. Add sand, water, plastic blocks, toy horses, and "dinosaurs-turned-fiery-dragons." These props will launch hours of fun!

Tips For An Extended Stay

Once your classroom centers are sparkling with fairy-tale magic, try these ideas for group time, outdoor fun, and parent involvement. Your young kings and queens may want to stay in the land of fairy tales forever!

Pam Crane

Once upon a time there was a queen and a king

All Together Now

Invite your group to work together to create a phenomenal fairy tale! Beginning with "Once upon a time," guide your group into choosing characters, a setting, and a plot for the tale. Record the story on a long length of white butcher paper; then invite youngsters to illustrate it. Once the characters are living happily ever after, invite your young authors and illustrators to sign their names at the end of the tale. Display the class story for all to see.

Out 'n' About

Every kingdom must have a royal treasure. Send your royal treasure hunters out to the playground to gather some loot. Of course, you'll want to have some treasure conveniently awaiting them! Use plastic eggs (spray-painted gold for a *really* fancy touch) as hiding places for colorful beads, shiny pennies, polished stones, or "golden" popcorn kernels. After they find the treasure, let them take turns hiding it all over again!

Hear Ye! Hear Ye!
You are invited to
A Royal Feast

where: Miss Stamey's Room

when: Friday at 12:00

Family Focus

Hear ye! Hear ye! Moms and dads are hereby invited to a royal feast! The castle staff is responsible for creating the menu, decorating the ballroom, and dressing in their finest fairy-tale costumes. Don't forget the classical music, and check out the table-setting tips on page 20. This grand event will be unforgettable—especially if you capture it on video!

Highlights Of Our Trip
Fun In Fairy-Tale Land

With a wink of an eye and the wave of a wand, we found ourselves right in the middle of a real live fairy tale—created and choreographed by *us!*

Visiting Plymouth Rock

Take a trip back in time to a place where the work and play of children centered around the natural resources of the land. Use treasures from the earth to introduce historical and cultural traditions, and to explore the many different ways natural materials are used. Your class will have a whole new way of looking at the great outdoors—and a better understanding of the Pilgrims and Native Americans of long ago.

ADMIT ONE

Getting Ready To Go!

When you're packing the time capsule for this trip back to the 1600s, look over the lists on page 27; then gather what you'll need based on the centers you choose. Below are a few more tips to help you prepare.

ADMIT ONE

Going On A Canoe Trip

If you can't find a real canoe, a refrigerator or dryer box will do! Seal the ends of the box; then turn it on its side and use a utility knife (when children aren't around) to carefully cut out a large oval from one side. If you can scavenge a couple of paddles, you'll be all set for little ones to hop in and paddle downstream!

Across The Atlantic

Make your classroom resemble Plymouth with a few agricultural props and a fabric sea. Several uncut yards of blue polyester will make a wonderful, rippling, and *inexpensive* Atlantic Ocean. Nearby, set out a big, shallow tub of sand. "Plant" some pumpkins and corn (with the husks on) in this Pilgrim's patch.

Tie-Dyeing

Ask each child to bring in a white T-shirt to tie-dye with natural cranberry dye. (See "What Happens When…" on page 32.)

Packing For Plymouth

Choose from the center ideas on pages 28–33. Here's a handy list of the supplies you'll need to prepare each one.

Art Area

Cranberry Creations: cranberries, electric frying pan, potato mashers, colander, paper, paintbrushes

Pumpkin-Patch Printing: miniature pumpkins, sharp knife (for teacher use), construction paper and/or butcher paper, tempera paint in autumn colors, shallow paint trays

Good-Earth Sculpting: blocks of wood, brown "plue," assorted natural materials

Wonderful Weaving: plastic lattice, thick yarns, strips of fabric, clothespins

Block Area

Going On A Canoe Trip: box canoe

It's A Village!: large appliance box and/or card table, blankets or sheets

Science Center

What Happens When…: white T-shirts, yarn, bucket, cranberry juice, red food coloring, vinegar, yellow or green food coloring (optional)

Writing Center

Special Names: paper, crayons, markers

At Plymouth Rock: paper, crayons, markers, large rock cutout (optional)

Dramatic-Play Center

Stocking The Ship: suitcases, dress-up clothing, maps, compass, telescope, play food

Setting The Table: baskets, small iron skillet, wooden utensils and bowls, clay flowerpots with saucers, small quilt

Preparing The Meal: Indian corn, pumpkins, gourds, uncolored play dough, rolling pins, pie pans, loaf pans

Music And Movement

Do You Hear What I Hear?: classroom objects to serve as drums and drumsticks

Sensory Tables And Tubs

Clay Play: moist clay, large tub, smocks

Pour In The Popcorn: large quantity of popcorn kernels, scoops, funnels

Pumpkins And Gourds: miniature pumpkins, small gourds

Reading Center

A Native American Book Nook: feathers, wooden beads, faux fur, large baskets or pottery pieces

Art Area

Fine-motor skills
Hand-eye coordination
Cognitive skills
Sorting
Patterning
Visual expression

Cranberry Creations

Make a natural dye for youngsters to explore. Cook two cups of cranberries in three to four cups of water in an electric frying pan until the berries are soft and somewhat runny. When the berries have cooled adequately, have children use potato mashers to squish them. Invite them to make potato-masher prints on paper. Then strain the berries through a colander and use the juice as paint!

Pumpkin-Patch Printing

For a seasonal takeoff on traditional apple printing, use pumpkins instead! Cut small pumpkins across the middle (saving the seeds for another day) so that children can hold onto the stems while they print. Put out large sheets of construction paper and autumn shades of tempera paint in shallow trays. For a class-sized pumpkin patch, let *everyone* make prints on a long length of bulletin-board paper or brown butcher paper.

Good-Earth Sculpting

Acquaint youngsters with the form and feel of natural materials with this open-ended art experience. For each of your young artists, supply a block of wood; some brown-tinted "plue" (see page 4); and an array of pinecones, gum balls (from a sweet gum tree), acorns, wooden beads, craft sticks, and feathers. Each child will create his own one-of-a-kind, good-earth masterpiece!

Wonderful Weaving

Introduce the basic concept of weaving by bringing in a section of plastic lattice. (A six- to eight-foot piece is available at your local home-improvement store for about $15.) Prop it between two small chairs, tucking the chair legs through holes in each end to secure it. Provide a basket of thick yarns and colorful strips of fabric. Clothespins clipped onto the ends of yarn lengths and fabric strips will make them easier for little hands to manipulate as they weave the material in, out, around, and through the holes in the lattice. When a child is finished, either have him "unweave" or just let the weaving grow and grow with the next visitors to this center.

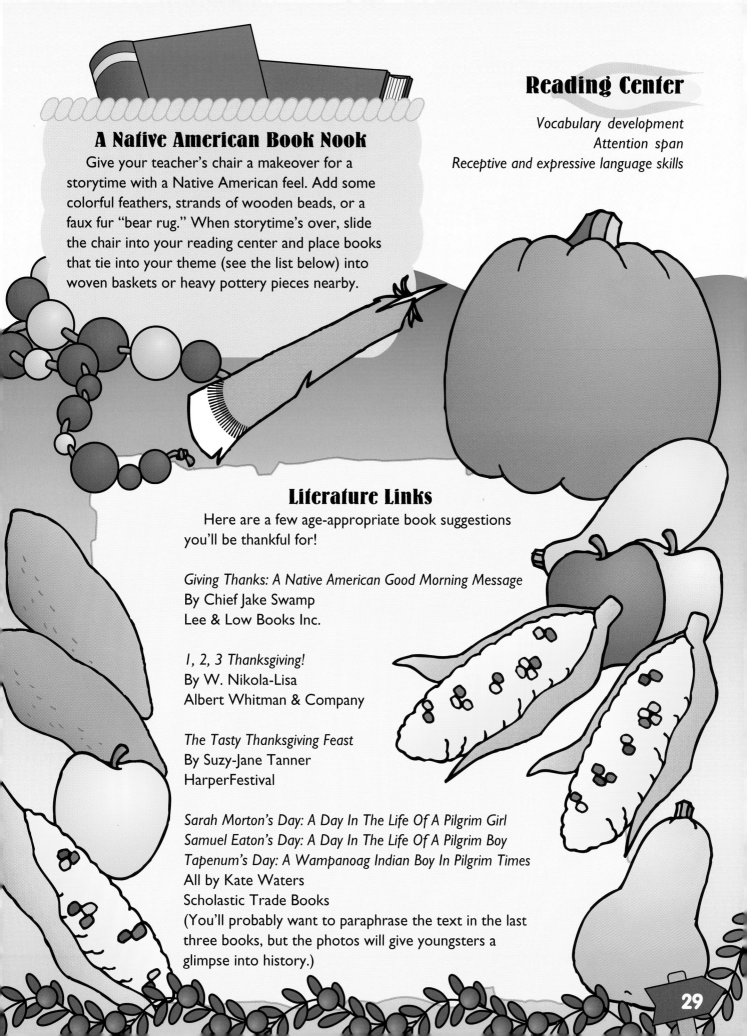

A Native American Book Nook

Give your teacher's chair a makeover for a storytime with a Native American feel. Add some colorful feathers, strands of wooden beads, or a faux fur "bear rug." When storytime's over, slide the chair into your reading center and place books that tie into your theme (see the list below) into woven baskets or heavy pottery pieces nearby.

Literature Links

Here are a few age-appropriate book suggestions you'll be thankful for!

Giving Thanks: A Native American Good Morning Message
By Chief Jake Swamp
Lee & Low Books Inc.

1, 2, 3 Thanksgiving!
By W. Nikola-Lisa
Albert Whitman & Company

The Tasty Thanksgiving Feast
By Suzy-Jane Tanner
HarperFestival

Sarah Morton's Day: A Day In The Life Of A Pilgrim Girl
Samuel Eaton's Day: A Day In The Life Of A Pilgrim Boy
Tapenum's Day: A Wampanoag Indian Boy In Pilgrim Times
All by Kate Waters
Scholastic Trade Books
(You'll probably want to paraphrase the text in the last three books, but the photos will give youngsters a glimpse into history.)

Dramatic-Play Center

Creative thinking
Verbal skills
Socialization

Stocking The Ship

Let's see....What will we need for a trip across the ocean? Provide some old suitcases, an assortment of clothes, maps, a compass, a telescope (real or make-believe), play food, and anything else you or your youngsters can think of to make the Pilgrims' voyage complete!

Setting The Table

Give your classroom kitchen a long-ago look. Pack up the plastic ware; then stock the home living area with baskets, a small iron skillet, and wooden utensils and bowls. Use small clay flowerpots and saucers as cups and plates. Add an old quilt for a quaint tablecloth.

Preparing The Meal

Make Indian corn, small pumpkins, and gourds the specialties of your Plymouth kitchen. Whip up a batch of your favorite play dough recipe minus the food coloring; then invite children to bake bread or make muffins and pies. Be sure to have rolling pins, pie plates, and loaf pans available for your Pilgrim bakers.

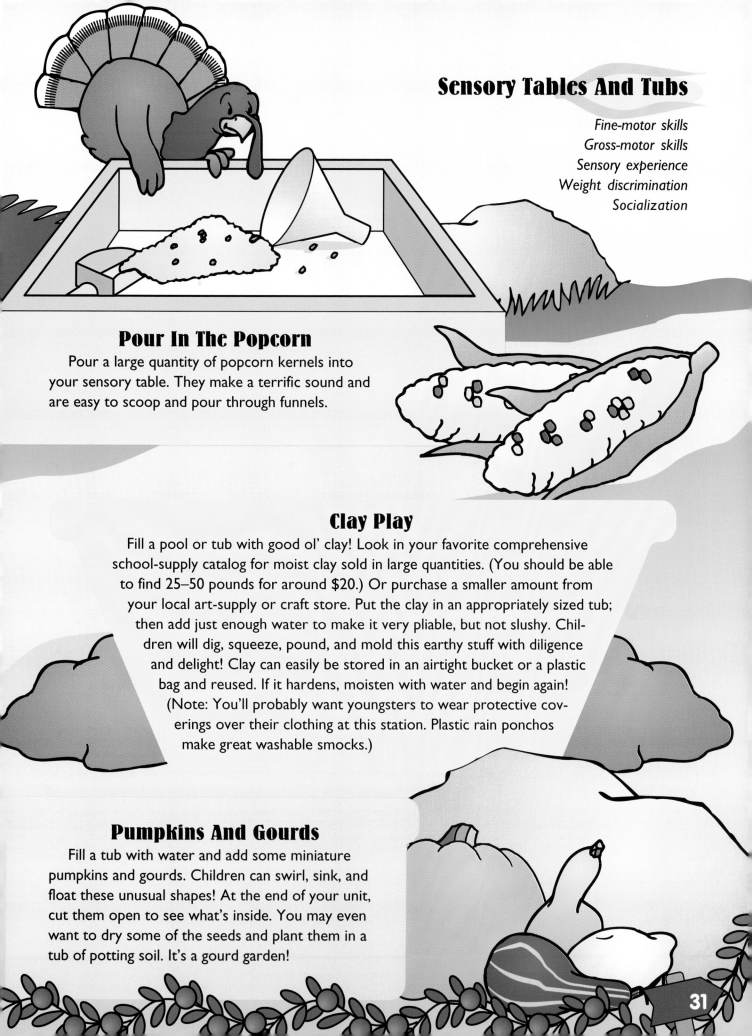

Sensory Tables And Tubs

Fine-motor skills
Gross-motor skills
Sensory experience
Weight discrimination
Socialization

Pour In The Popcorn

Pour a large quantity of popcorn kernels into your sensory table. They make a terrific sound and are easy to scoop and pour through funnels.

Clay Play

Fill a pool or tub with good ol' clay! Look in your favorite comprehensive school-supply catalog for moist clay sold in large quantities. (You should be able to find 25–50 pounds for around $20.) Or purchase a smaller amount from your local art-supply or craft store. Put the clay in an appropriately sized tub; then add just enough water to make it very pliable, but not slushy. Children will dig, squeeze, pound, and mold this earthy stuff with diligence and delight! Clay can easily be stored in an airtight bucket or a plastic bag and reused. If it hardens, moisten with water and begin again! (Note: You'll probably want youngsters to wear protective coverings over their clothing at this station. Plastic rain ponchos make great washable smocks.)

Pumpkins And Gourds

Fill a tub with water and add some miniature pumpkins and gourds. Children can swirl, sink, and float these unusual shapes! At the end of your unit, cut them open to see what's inside. You may even want to dry some of the seeds and plant them in a tub of potting soil. It's a gourd garden!

Science Center

Color and pattern recognition
Exploring cause and effect
Socialization

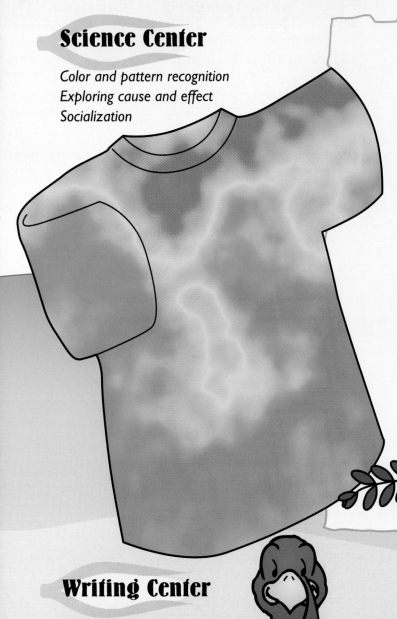

What Happens When...

Have each child bring a plain white T-shirt to school to tie-dye with cranberry juice! Tie each shirt in several knots. Wrap a long piece of yarn tightly around each shirt, so children can lower their shirts into a bucket of cranberry dye and then retrieve them.

To make the dye, first create a mixture of one gallon of cranberry juice and a hearty splash of red food coloring. Then add two cups of vinegar to this mixture. To make a brighter dye, add a few drops of yellow food coloring. For an earthy tone, add a few drops of green. Have each child dip her knotted shirt into the bucket of dye, then pull it out. Dry the shirts overnight; then untie them and allow them to dry further, if necessary. This dye is only semipermanent, but 100 percent fun!

(Note: This is best done as an outdoor activity.)

Writing Center

Auditory skills
Verbal skills
Creative thinking
Word association
Writing
Socialization

At Plymouth Rock

Encourage each child to draw and dictate a story about what it would have been like to be at Plymouth Rock for the first Thanksgiving. Would they have played tag? Eaten popcorn? Helped Mom and Dad wash all the dishes? If desired, display the children's stories around a giant rock cut from gray or tan paper and titled "If We Were At Plymouth Rock..."

Special Names

Native American tradition holds that children are given names that describe something about them, and this custom is practiced in many other cultures of the world as well. Discuss this custom and give some examples to help your students understand. Then invite each child to create his own special name that he feels describes him. On a separate sheet of paper, write each child's newly created name and his dictation as to why he chose it. Invite him to illustrate his page with a self-portrait. Bind the pages into a class book. Youngsters will want to read about themselves over and over again!

Going On A Canoe Trip

Bring out the appliance box you've transformed into a swift canoe (see page 26). Young builders can then transform the block area into a river's surroundings and paddle past mountains and valleys. Or perhaps they'd like to pretend this box canoe is the mighty *Mayflower* and they are the Pilgrims arriving at Plymouth. We'd better get busy building some shelters!

(see page 26)

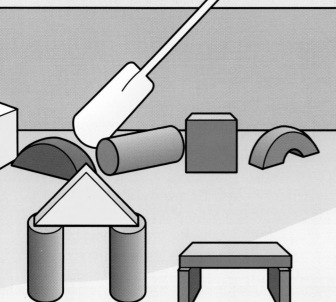

Block Area

Gross-motor skills
Problem-solving skills
Socialization

It's A Village!

Transform your block area into a Pilgrim settlement. Bring in a large appliance box, a foldout card table, or even a pair of sturdy chairs to use as house "frames." Add a few lightweight blankets or sheets. Your young settlers will know exactly what to do!

Music And Movement

Auditory skills
Patterning
Echoing
Socialization

Do You Hear What I Hear?

Nothing beats a drum—except a homemade one! Invite your students to help you look around your classroom for objects that could serve as drums or drumsticks. For example, rubber spatulas make friendly drumsticks. They tap out a beat, yet keep the noise down. How about a shoebox drum? Once you've found some drum and drumstick substitutes, add them to your music center. Encourage children in this center to create their own patterns of rhythm and to echo the patterns tapped out by friends.

33

Tips For An Extended Stay

Enjoy the Early American experience beyond your centers with these ideas for a collaborative project, outdoor play, and parent involvement.

All Together Now

Invite your youngsters to communicate as the Native Americans did at Plymouth—through pictures and symbols. Ask children to brainstorm some simple symbols that they could use to tell about a typical school day. Get them started with some examples, such as a drawing of a slide to mean "playground" or a picture of a milk carton to mean "lunchtime." Assist them in writing a group symbol story about their day at school. See? Writing's easy!

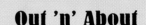

Out 'n' About

The setting is Plymouth Rock....Well, okay, the setting is really your playground, but you can make it *look* like Plymouth Rock! Tie a white sheet to your swing set or jungle gym for a makeshift *Mayflower*. Scatter some shells on the "beach" nearby. Put some toy gardening tools and popcorn kernels in the sandbox and you have the Pilgrims' planting area. Build a "campfire" and bring out an iron skillet and some ears of maize. If you made the canoe described in "Going On A Canoe Trip" (page 26), bring it outdoors, too! Once you've set the stage, your young Pilgrims and Native Americans will create the plot.

Family Focus

After your youngsters have explored the first Thanksgiving at Plymouth, invite parents to share in the fun! Encourage parent-and-child playtime at the centers you've set up; then sit down as a group to discuss Thanksgiving then and now. Have family members share their special family traditions for celebrating Thanksgiving. Finish up the day by enjoying a feast of foods that children at Plymouth Rock might have eaten—corn bread, cranberry muffins, apple cider, dried fruit, corn on the cob, and other veggies.

Highlights Of Our Trip
Visiting Plymouth Rock

Have you ever sailed on the *Mayflower,* paddled a canoe, or baked bread in a Pilgrim's kitchen? *We have!* Look at all the fun we had on our trip to Plymouth Rock—and we never even left school!

Home, Sweet Home

This journey takes children to their favorite place of all—home! The activities in this unit are designed to give children an opportunity to share something special about their families and to learn about the friends they spend a *lot* of time with—their classmates. So celebrate both diversity and sameness as you explore family work, play, and living day to day!

A House For Me!

Turn an appliance box into a house (or condo) for your block area (see "The House That *We* Built!" on page 42). Use a utility knife (when children aren't around) to cut windows and doors from the box. Bring in a welcome mat for an extra homey touch. Write each child's address on a separate sheet of construction paper. Periodically change the house address throughout your unit.

3515 West Market St.

WELCOME

ADMIT ONE

ADMIT ONE

Getting Ready To Go!

Bringing a sense of home to the classroom will require some special touches and special materials. Check out the lists on page 37; then gather the supplies you'll need according to the centers you choose. Use the ideas below to help you further prepare for your trip home.

Wanted: Photos

Collect photos from each family, including current and baby photos of children. Use some of the photos for "Then And Now" on page 42. Put the rest in a photo album to spark discussions about family.

Dear Family:
    Our next trip is to a place we all love—home! Can you help us get ready by sending some photos of your child (a baby photo and a more current one)? Also, please send in a can or box of one of your child's favorite (nonperishable) foods.
    Thanks a bunch!
    Miss Eileen

And While You're Asking...

And as long as you're requesting items to make your unit complete, ask each family to send in dress-up clothes and favorite nonperishable foods for use in the dramatic-play center (see the activities on page 40).

Touches Of Home

Choose from the center ideas on pages 38–43. Here's a handy list of the supplies you'll need to prepare each one.

Art Area

Family Portraits: heavy construction paper or small poster boards, skin-toned markers, collage materials, glue

Picture Frames: paper plates, overhead projector transparency frames, craft sticks, crayons, paint, glue, collage materials

Home Is Where The Art Is: sturdy cardboard pieces, collage materials, glue, paper, markers

Reading Center

A Touch Of Home: items from your home (photos, pillows, plants, etc.)

Dramatic-Play Center

Dress-Ups From Home: clothing and accessories donated by families; trunk, dresser, or box

What's For Dinner?: nonperishable food items donated by families

Music And Movement

In The Neighborhood: colored Con-Tact® paper, children's school photos (optional), recorded music

Sensory Tables And Tubs

A Bubble Bath: bubble bath, rubber ducks, washcloths, bath towels

Mix And Match: socks of many colors and sizes, clothesline, clothespins

"Kazoodles" Of Noodles: dried macaroni noodles, soup pots, ladles

Whose Turn Is It Tonight?: dish detergent, dish scrubbers, plastic dishes, dish towels, dish rack

Writing Center

Things In My House: magazines, scissors, large sheet of tagboard, glue sticks, marker

All In The Family: paper, crayons, pillow or throw blanket, lamp

Science Center

Then And Now: photos donated by families, tray

Block Area

The House That We Built!: box house, children's hard hats, tape measures, sandpaper, levels, house-painting brushes, set of blueprints (optional)

Art Area

Visual expression
Cognitive skills
Fine-motor skills
Color and shape recognition
Socialization

Family Portraits

You'll be amazed at the wonderful portraits your preschoolers come up with! Provide sheets of heavy construction paper or small poster boards to use as backgrounds for this collage project. Supply markers in different skin tones and plenty of collage materials, such as construction paper, a variety of yarn for hair, small fabric scraps, buttons, ribbon, and anything else you can find! Hang the finished works in your own classroom portrait gallery.

Picture Frames

Picture frames abound in most homes, and the very best ones are those made by little hands! Children can draw, paint, or glue colorful treasures onto frames of various shapes. Just stock your center with the following:

— For circular frames, use various sizes of paper plates with the centers cut out.
— For rectangular frames, use overhead projector transparency frames.
— For square frames, use hot glue to construct frames from wide or skinny wooden craft sticks.

Home Is Where The Art Is

Offer a variety of art materials, such as craft sticks, scraps of bulletin-board border and construction paper, plain or colored toothpicks, coffee stirring sticks, and dyed macaroni. Give each artist a sturdy cardboard base and invite him to create a collage rendering of his home with some touches of glue and creativity. Display each finished home collage with a label showing the child's name and address.

Brett
1607 Cady Lane

A Touch Of Home

Go the extra mile and bring in some special things from *your* home. After all, teachers don't *really* live at school! Add to your reading area a special quilt or afghan, photos from your nightstand, an embroidered pillow, or a favorite plant. Let your preschoolers feel the special touch you give to your own family as they settle in to read.

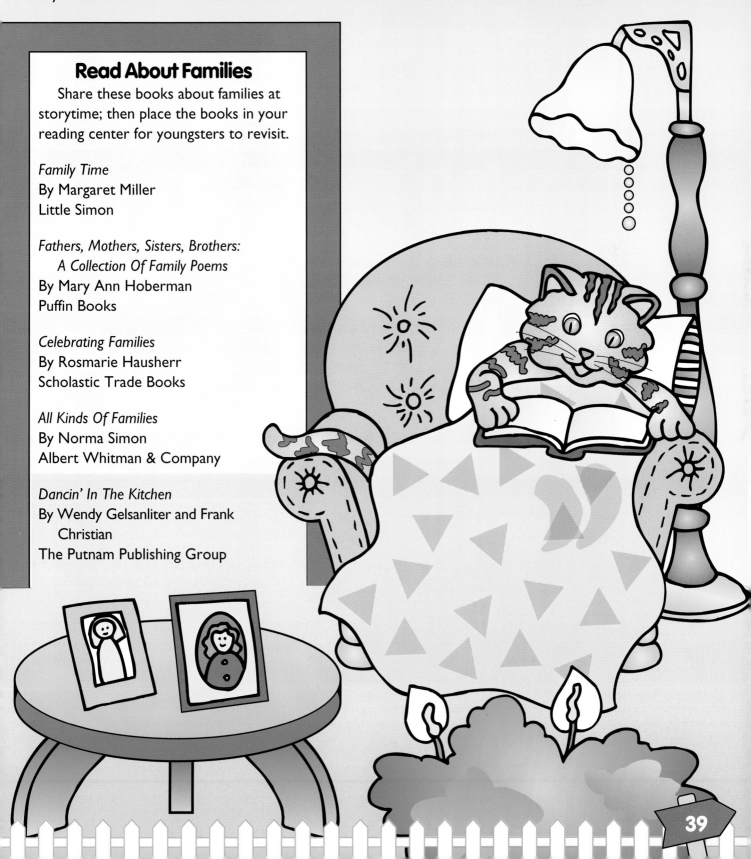

Reading Center

Vocabulary development
Attention span
Receptive and expressive language skills

Read About Families

Share these books about families at storytime; then place the books in your reading center for youngsters to revisit.

Family Time
By Margaret Miller
Little Simon

Fathers, Mothers, Sisters, Brothers: A Collection Of Family Poems
By Mary Ann Hoberman
Puffin Books

Celebrating Families
By Rosmarie Hausherr
Scholastic Trade Books

All Kinds Of Families
By Norma Simon
Albert Whitman & Company

Dancin' In The Kitchen
By Wendy Gelsanliter and Frank Christian
The Putnam Publishing Group

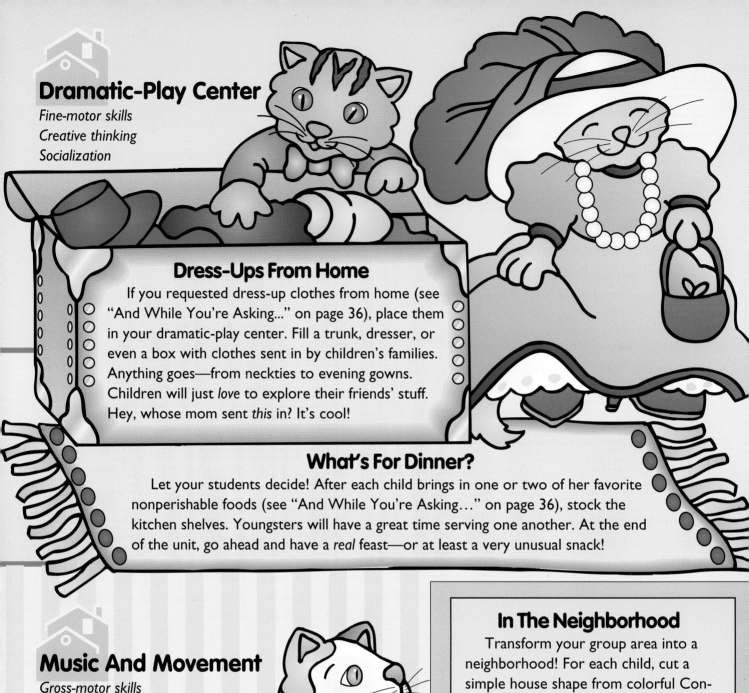

Dramatic-Play Center

Fine-motor skills
Creative thinking
Socialization

Dress-Ups From Home

If you requested dress-up clothes from home (see "And While You're Asking..." on page 36), place them in your dramatic-play center. Fill a trunk, dresser, or even a box with clothes sent in by children's families. Anything goes—from neckties to evening gowns. Children will just *love* to explore their friends' stuff. Hey, whose mom sent *this* in? It's cool!

What's For Dinner?

Let your students decide! After each child brings in one or two of her favorite nonperishable foods (see "And While You're Asking…" on page 36), stock the kitchen shelves. Youngsters will have a great time serving one another. At the end of the unit, go ahead and have a *real* feast—or at least a very unusual snack!

Music And Movement

Gross-motor skills
Spatial awareness
Listening skills
Socialization

In The Neighborhood

Transform your group area into a neighborhood! For each child, cut a simple house shape from colorful Con-Tact® paper. Add the child's duplicated school photo and/or name to the cut-out. Peel the backing off the Con-Tact® paper and stick the houses to the floor in your group area. Play some music and encourage your little ones to step from house to house, visiting their "neighbors." Stop the music and have each child stop on a house. Children love to see whose house they end up on!

Alan   Linda   Sammy   Kerrance   Shawnda

Sensory Tables And Tubs

Sensory discrimination
Fine-motor skills
Gross-motor skills
Color, shape, and size recognition
Socialization

A Bubble Bath

Doesn't *everybody* love a bubble bath? Create your own in a sensory table with the children's favorite brand of bubbles. Throw in a few rubber duckies and some washcloths for fun. Have a few bath towels nearby for drippy hands.

Mix And Match

Fill a sensory table or laundry basket with *lots* of socks to sort! Be sure to have all different sizes, ranging from teeny-tiny baby socks to adult extra large ones. String a clothesline nearby and provide clothespins so children can hang up the pairs they find.

"Kazoodles" Of Noodles

Is it soup yet? Fill a tub with plain or dyed macaroni (uncooked). Add some big soup pots and ladles—but only *pretend* water. Lunch will be ready in a jiffy! (*Tip: When you're finished with this center, add the pasta to your art area.*)

Whose Turn Is It Tonight?

Well, here's something all families have in common: *Somebody* has to wash those dishes! Fill your water table with warm water, a little dish detergent, dish scrubbers, and lots of "dirty" plastic dishes! Supply dish towels and a rubber dish rack on a table nearby for a true-to-life accent. Believe it or not, this station is a favorite!

Science Center

Analytical thinking
Sorting
Visual discrimination
Socialization

Then And Now

Gather the family photos you requested (see "Wanted: Photos" on page 36). For each child, choose a baby picture and a more current photo. Place these photos on a tray for comparing and matching. Can students match all the baby pictures to the more recent photos? Ask them to describe how they made some of their matches. Invite children to discuss the changes that have taken place since babyhood and to celebrate how much they've grown.

Block Area

Gross-motor skills
Counting
Sequencing
Problem solving
Socialization

The House That We Built!

Bring out the box house, 'cause it's time to get busy building! (See "A House For Me!" on page 36.) Supply your young home builders with hard hats, tape measures, sandpaper, levels, and big house-painting brushes (with imaginary, invisible paint, of course). Your block area will become a neighborhood in no time at all! For a fun touch, provide authentic blueprints borrowed from an architect or engineer.

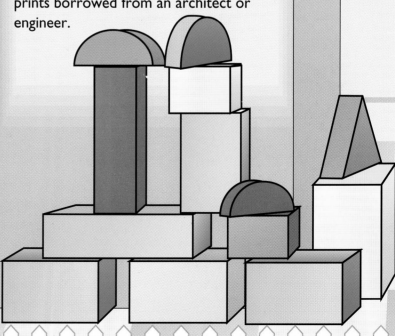

Writing Center

Auditory skills
Verbal skills
Word association
Writing
Socialization

Things In My House

Picture this! Have your class create a magazine-picture collage to tell about their homes or spark stories of home and family. Have each child cut pictures from magazines of things found in her house—furniture, foods, people, pets, etc. Give each child a glue stick and invite her to stick her pictures onto a large sheet of tagboard. Write each child's dictation near her pictures or simply use the resulting mural to jump-start stories straight from your children's imaginations. "There was a cat who liked to sleep on top of the refrigerator...."

All In The Family

Encourage children to dictate and draw stories about their families. Provide construction-paper pages cut into simple house shapes. For a special story sharing time, set up an author's chair to resemble a comfy chair from home—perhaps a pillow or a throw blanket will do the trick. Click on a cozy lamp for a real homey feel. Then invite each young author to have a seat and share his story.

Tips For An Extended Stay

After you've brought that feeling of home to your classroom centers, try extending this theme with these ideas for a group activity, outdoor play, and family fun.

All Together Now

Home is a wonderful place! But what about those who don't have a home? Here's a perfect opportunity to build youngsters' awareness of others and help them develop empathy. After discussing the plight of the homeless, involve your children in baking a batch of basic sugar cookies. Invite them to frost and decorate the cookies with lots of colorful sprinkles. As a group, deliver these sweet treats to a local homeless shelter.

Out 'n' About

Choose a day when the forecast is for fine weather. Then invite each child to bring an outdoor toy from home to school for the day. Roller skates, riding toys, and balls are twice the fun when you share them with a classmate!

Family Focus

Preschoolers *love* to talk about their families! Why not have children bring their parents for show-and-tell throughout the unit? They can read or tell a favorite story, show clips of home videos, share with the class about their jobs or hobbies, or cook a special snack from a secret family recipe.

Highlights Of Our Trip
Home, Sweet Home

From sea to shining sea, there's one place we love the best—*home!* We discovered that our families are the same in many ways, and yet uniquely different! Here's a bit about what we did.

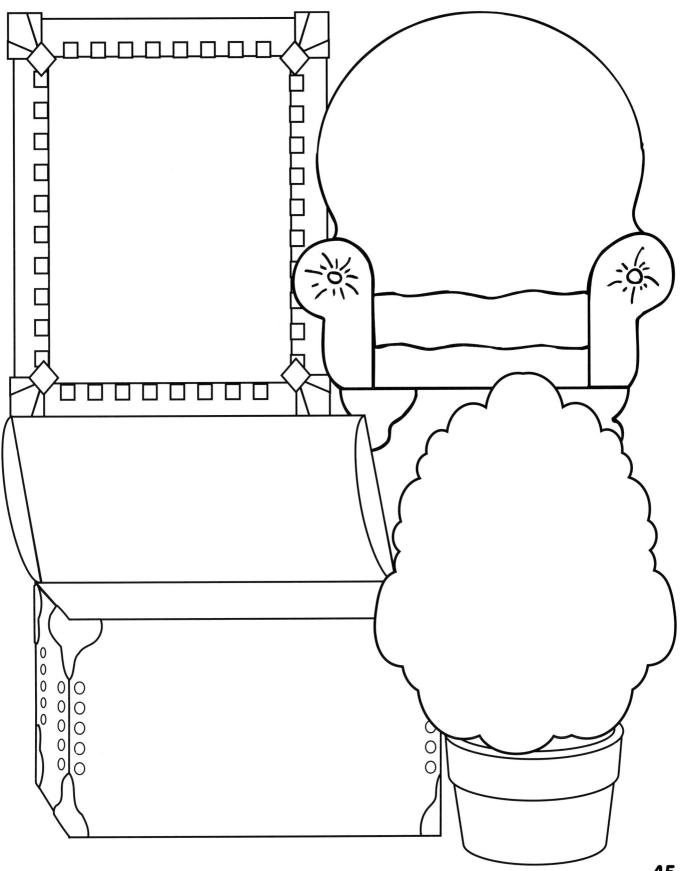

A Winter Wonderland

Bundle up and head for a magical environment with hands-on activities to help little ones explore snow, ice, and cold temperatures. Brrr!

Getting Ready To Go!

Before you pull on your mittens and slip into your snow boots, ready the materials you'll need for the centers of your choice (see the lists on page 47). Then check out the cool ideas below to help you prepare for your snowy expedition.

ADMIT ONE

ADMIT ONE

Be A Box Collector

You'll need a couple of big boxes for some of the center ideas that follow. Transform a large, flat box into a fireplace for "Reading By The Fire" on page 49. To create an Arctic hideaway (see "A Comfy, Cozy Igloo" on page 53), use a utility knife (when children aren't around) to cut an arched doorway in one side of a dryer box. Then have youngsters finish it up using the directions on page 53.

Cold-Weather Clothing

Send home a note asking parents to donate old winter clothing and winter sports gear for your dramatic-play center. (See "Bundle Up!" on page 50.)

Imaginary Ice

Cut some chunks of Styrofoam® "ice" to add to the atmosphere and for use with "Watch Out For Glaciers!" on page 51 and "A Comfy, Cozy Igloo" on page 53. Just gather some large pieces of Styrofoam® packing; then use a utility knife to cut them into chunks.

Stock Up For Winter

Choose from the center ideas on pages 48–53. Here's a handy list of the supplies you'll need to prepare each one.

Art Area

Cool Colors: silver, blue, purple, and white collage materials; white tagboard or construction paper; glue sticks or "plue"

Windy Wands: ribbon, strips of blue or opalescent cellophane, packing tape

It's A Blizzard!: sheet of black plastic or black plastic trash bags, tape, newspaper, white tempera paint, shaving cream, rubber spatulas, squeegees, black construction paper

Snow Flurries: white crayons, white paper plates, blue-tinted water, paintbrushes

Dramatic-Play Center

Bundle Up!: winter clothing donated by families, suitcase

Music And Movement

It's A Skating Rink!: nine-inch aluminum pie plates, slow instrumental music, "Windy Wands" (page 48)

Reading Center

Reading By The Fire: large box, paints and paintbrush, pillows or braided rug, children's slippers

Block Area

A Comfy, Cozy Igloo: box igloo, chunks of Styrofoam®, glue, blanket or sleeping bag

Ice Fishing: tagboard fish, paper clips, magnetic fishing pole, bucket, skillet, spatula, paper plates

Sensory Tables And Tubs

Watch Out For Glaciers!: chunks of Styrofoam®, Styrofoam® packing peanuts, big plastic spoons or sand shovels

Ice Is Nice: ice, metal and wooden bowls, mittens

Snow Dough: uncolored play dough, opalescent glitter or confetti

Windy And Wonderful: cellophane streamers, tongs, metal or clear plastic bowls

Science Center

Rainbows On Ice: containers of blue, red, and yellow water; pans and molds; tubs; rock salt

Writing Center

Indoor Snow: paper, crayons, markers

Snowfriends: white paper cut into snowman shapes, crayons

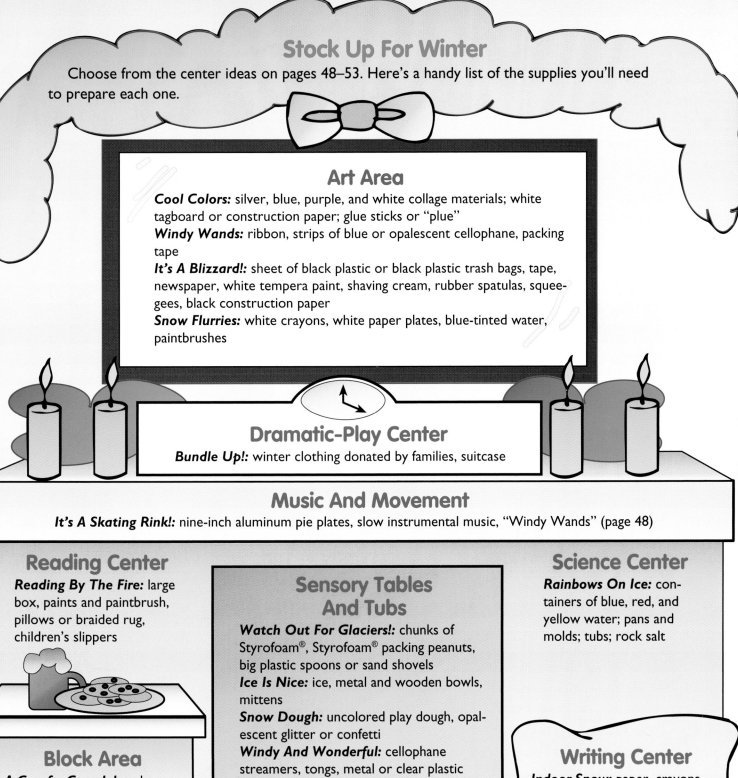

Art Area

Fine-motor skills
Hand-eye coordination
Cognitive skills
Color and shape recognition

Cool Colors

Offer a variety of silver, blue, purple, and white materials for creating wintry collages. Provide large sheets of white tagboard or construction paper, as well as glue sticks or "plue" (see page 4).

Snow Flurries

Magical snow scenes will appear when youngsters use this crayon-resist technique. Have a child use white crayon to draw snowflakes on a white paper plate. When the old North Wind blows in (blue-tinted water applied with a paintbrush), flurries will appear!

Windy Wands

These wonderful wands are fun to make and fun to use, too! Provide a variety of ribbon and strips of blue or opalescent cellophane. Have each child choose several strips of cellophane or ribbon in the colors of her choice. Have her gather the ribbon and cellophane into a bundle, then stick the ends onto a long piece of packing tape. Then have her roll the tape around and around the ribbon ends to create a handle.

It's A Blizzard!

Cover a table with a sheet of black plastic or a few cut-open black plastic trash bags. Tape the edges of the plastic to the table to prevent slipping. Use newspaper to protect the floor below the table. Then pour a mixture of white tempera paint and shaving cream onto the plastic to represent snow. Give children rubber spatulas and squeegees with which to paint. To make a snowy print, press a sheet of black construction paper onto the design, rub, and then carefully peel the paper up.

Stories For A Snowy Day

Blanket your reading area with snow-related books. And invite youngsters to drift on over for a snowy tale at storytime. Here are some cool choices!

Snowballs
By Lois Ehlert
Harcourt Brace & Company

The First Snowfall
By Anne and Harlow Rockwell
Aladdin Paperbacks

Winter
By Chris L. Demarest
Harcourt Brace & Company

The Snowy Day
By Ezra Jack Keats
Viking Press

Rainsong/Snowsong
By Philemon Sturges
North-South Books Inc.

When Winter Comes
By Robert Maass
Henry Holt And Company, Inc.

Reading By The Fire

What better place to cuddle up with a good book on a snowy day than by a roaring fire? Paint a big box to resemble a fireplace with a cheery fire. Set the box against a wall in your reading area; then add a braided rug or some cozy pillows and a couple of pairs of children's slippers. Ahhhh!

Dramatic-Play Center

Creative thinking
Verbal skills
Fine-motor skills
Socialization

Music And Movement

Gross-motor skills
Auditory skills
Creative thinking
Socialization

Bundle Up!

Gather up the clothing parents have sent in (see "Cold-Weather Clothing" on page 46). Toss it all into a suitcase in your dramatic-play center. Old scarves, mittens, boots, ski bibs, jackets, and goggles will transform your youngsters into skiers, sledders, and skaters extraordinaire! Take advantage of this opportunity to observe little ones' proficiency with fasteners, such as snaps, zippers, and buttons.

It's A Skating Rink!

Make your own skating rink—right in the middle of your classroom! You'll need a box full of nine-inch aluminum pie plates (shiny silver ice skates), some room to move, and a recording of slow instrumental music. Bring over some "Windy Wands" (page 48) to add to the creative expression. Children will swirl and glide like magic—even without ice!

Sensory Tables And Tubs

Tactile discrimination
Fine-motor skills
Gross-motor skills
Socialization

Snow Dough

Triple your favorite play dough recipe, omitting the color and adding opalescent glitter or confetti. Fill a tub with this sparkling snow dough and your little ones can make snow sculptures without ever going outside!

Ice Is Nice

Fill a tub with ice. Add both metal and wooden bowls. Have mittens available for children to wear as they explore. Which is colder—a metal bowl or a wooden one?

Watch Out For Glaciers!

Float big chunks of Styrofoam® in your water table (see "Imaginary Ice" on page 46). For a contrast in size, add Styrofoam® packing peanuts. Toss in some big plastic spoons or sand shovels for youngsters to use as snow scoopers.

Windy And Wonderful

Can you catch the North Wind? Well, *almost!* Fill a tub or pool with cellophane streamers (the same type used for "Windy Wands" on page 48). Add tongs and shiny metal or clear bowls. This is a soothing sensory interaction. Place the tub or pool on the floor, and some of your youngsters may just hop right in!

Writing Center

Creative language and thought processing
Word association
Writing
Socialization

Indoor Snow

What a silly-willy weather day! It's snowing *inside* instead of out! What will we do? Make snowmen on the tables? Dig tunnels through the block area? Add sugar and cream and have a snow snack? Create a class story that sparkles with your youngsters' imagination and captures the unpredictable nature of snow.

Terri

My snowman friend and I watch TV together.

One day it snowed in our classroom! We made a snowman and a snowlady in the reading center. We had to wear our coats and hats. The snow lady read us a story!

Snowfriends

What if a real live snowman came to play at your house one day? What would you do? What games would you play? Would he stay for supper? Would he live at your house forever? Provide white paper cut into simple snowman shapes and invite your young authors to tell you all about their imaginary snowfriends.

Science Center

Analytical thinking
Temperature discrimination
Color discrimination

Rainbows On Ice

Explore a different kind of watercolor when you set up this freeze-and-melt center. Tint separate containers of water blue, red, and yellow. Pour the colored water into pans and molds of various sizes and shapes before freezing. Place two primary colors of ice into a tub, add a sprinkle or two of rock salt, and have little ones watch and stir to see what happens.

A Comfy, Cozy Igloo

Pull out the dryer box and the Styrofoam® blocks you've prepared (see "Imaginary Ice" and "Be A Box Collector" on page 46). Encourage your students to glue the Styrofoam® shapes onto the box to create an igloo look-alike. Throw a warm blanket or a sleeping bag inside, and your preschoolers are ready for a stay in the Arctic! It may not look *exactly* like the structures you'd see in the far north, but your kids will love it!

Ice Fishing

Right next door to the igloo, set up an ice-fishing hole. Just cut a supply of tagboard fish and attach a paper clip to each one. Make a fishing pole by attaching a length of yarn to a yardstick or dowel and tying a magnet to the free end. Have little ones build a campfire from blocks so they can cook their catch. Provide a bucket for collecting fish, a skillet and spatula for frying them, and paper plates for serving them up!

Tips For An Extended Stay

Once your centers are filled with frosty fun, try these ideas for a collaborative project, outdoor play, and parent involvement.

Out 'n' About

Winter isn't the same everywhere you go. See if your children can detect signs of winter in *your* area. Head outdoors for a scavenger hunt. Guide children to note changes in plants and trees, birds' nests, insects, and animals. Equip each hunter with a small magnifying glass to help her uncover some clues to winter!

Family Focus

Ask parents to join you for a field trip to the nearest ice-skating rink. Take a camera, because you'll definitely want photos of *this!* Upon returning to your classroom, serve everyone a treat—hot chocolate with snowy whipped cream. Mmmm!

All Together Now

Invite your class to concoct their own edible snow village on a big foil-covered table. Provide marshmallows, marshmallow cream or vanilla pudding, coconut, and lots of colorful toothpicks. Throw in a few gumdrops for good measure. You won't be able to display this creation for long, so be sure to snap a few pictures before it "melts"!

Highlights Of Our Trip
A Winter Wonderland

What's white, wet, and wonderful? Snow, snow, snow! Bundle up and come see how we brought winter inside.

Adventure In The Jungle

Grab your hat, slip on your boots, and don't forget your umbrella, 'cause you're going to venture into the thick tropical rain forest! While you're there, you'll dance to the rhythm of rain sticks, collect some crawling critters, scoop up quicksand, and plant a jungle of your very own.

Getting Ready To Go!

Prepare for your jungle adventure by gathering the provisions you'll need to create each center you choose (see the lists on page 57). Then create a few items that will help transform your classroom into a deep green jungle—just ready to be explored!

Furry Feet

Find the cheapest place in town to buy fuzzy slippers; then stock up on a few large pairs. Add claws by cutting out felt triangles and attaching them with fabric glue, clear fingernail polish, or your hot-glue gun. Children will want to wear these year-round!

Jungle-Jammin' Instruments

Create these simple rhythm instruments to bring the sounds of the tropics to life.

Rain Shakers

Half-fill clear, plastic soft-drink bottles with colorful rice. As a variation, put rice or beans into colored plastic eggs; then seal the eggs shut with a hot-glue gun. These are perfect for little hands.

Rain Sticks

To make a rain stick, use diluted glue (one part water to two parts glue) to cover a paper-towel tube with colorful tissue-paper squares. When the glue is dry, cover one end of the tube with colored duct tape; then pour lentils inside. Tape over the other end. To play, tilt the tube from end to end, letting the lentils fall through the tube.

Rhythm Sticks

Cover a pair of paper-towel tubes as described above, but omit the lentils and duct tape. These sturdy sticks will last and last.

Special Provisions

Choose from the center ideas on pages 58–63. Here's a handy list of the supplies you'll need to prepare each one.

Art Area

Now That's A Snake!: small paper plates, watercolors, stapler or hole puncher, yarn
Clay Creatures: clay, coffee stirrers, plastic beads, craft feathers, colored pasta, green Easter grass, gum balls from a sweet-gum tree (optional)
Picture Perfect: magazines, scissors, clear Con-Tact® paper, real greenery or green Easter grass

Reading Center

Storytime Seat: real or silk greenery, silk flowers, stuffed toy jungle animal, straw hat, sunglasses

Writing Center

On A Jungle Walk: chart paper, markers
Snaky Stories: snakes cut from bulletin-board paper, crayons

Dramatic-Play Center

Fruits Of The Tropics: tropical fruits donated by families, baskets, wooden bowls and utensils

Block Area

Happy Habitat: stuffed toy jungle animals or pictures of jungle animals, toilet-tissue-tube binoculars, broken or toy camera, bamboo branches or large houseplant

Sensory Tables And Tubs

Quicksand!: cornstarch, food coloring, putty knives, wooden spoons
The Swamplands: green Easter grass; pasta forks, tongs, or rubber spatulas; rubber fishing worms
Jungle Puddles: blue and green food coloring, sequins, aquarium nets

Science Center

Hey, There's A Jungle In Here!: potting soil, birdseed, watering cans, large spoons, sheet of plastic, magnifying glasses
Scents Of The Rain Forest: extracts and corresponding foods (pineapple, coconut, vanilla, and banana), cotton balls, salt shakers or bowls, boxes or pictures of foods made from tropical fruit

Music And Movement

Jungle Moods: recording of rain forest sounds, rhythm instruments
Furry Feet Dance To The Beat: fuzzy-slipper animal feet

Art Area

Visual expression
Fine-motor skills
Hand-eye coordination
Color recognition
Shape recognition

Now *That's* A Snake!

Invite children to create the most beautiful snake *ever* with small paper plates and watercolor paints. After each child has painted a plate, staple the plates together to form a snake. Or, for a more fluid look, hole-punch opposite sides of each plate and connect them together with short lengths of yarn. Hang the finished snake from your ceiling, around a pole, or across a bulletin board.

Clay Creatures

Bring out the clay, coffee stirring sticks (cut to various lengths), small plastic beads, pipe cleaners, craft feathers, colored pasta, and green Easter grass. And if you have a bunch of those pesky gum balls from a sweet-gum tree, toss those in, too! Then have youngsters construct unusual jungle creatures and tropical insects using the materials. Encourage them to use the Easter grass as silly fur or as a nest for a clay creature.

Picture Perfect

Make a realistic mural for your classroom rain forest. Have children cut pictures of animals, insects, and fish from nature magazines. Then lay a long sheet of clear Con-Tact® paper sticky side up on a table. Invite the children to stick their cutouts (picture side down) onto the paper. Add some real greenery (gathered on a nature walk or brought from home). Or use green Easter grass as a substitute. Before you know it, you'll have a lush version of the tropics ready to be seen by all!

Reading Center

Vocabulary development
Attention span
Receptive and expressive language skills

Storytime Seat

Get ready to redecorate the favorite seat in the house—your teacher's chair! Add as much green foliage as you can find (real or *almost real*), some vibrant silk flowers, and perhaps a stuffed parrot, monkey, or other toy jungle critter to use as a prop. A straw hat and a pair of sunglasses are all you need to set the stage for a journey through the jungle! When storytime's over, slide the chair into the reading area so little ones can kick back with a book from the list below.

Jungle Books

Whether you're looking for a delightful story or informative illustrations of jungle animals, this list will make your safari to the library a little easier!

Rumble In The Jungle
By Giles Andreae
Published by Little Tiger Press

Who Is The Beast?
By Keith Baker
Published by Voyager Picture Books

Rainforest Animals
By Paul Hess
Published by De Agostini Editions Ltd.

Amazon Alphabet
By Tanis Jordan
Published by Kingfisher

Dramatic-Play Center

Creative thinking
Verbal skills
Counting
Sorting
Socialization

Fruits Of The Tropics

Mmmmm…pineapples, coconuts, mangoes, papayas, and star fruit! These incredible edibles are some of the best parts of the jungle! Ask parents to send in some of these fresh fruits for youngsters to explore and play with in your dramatic-play center. Big baskets, wooden bowls, and wooden utensils are the perfect props to add.

Music And Movement

Auditory discrimination
Rhythm
Gross-motor skills
Socialization

Jungle Moods

Add an authentic touch to your environment by playing recordings of rain forest sounds. (Check your local library or bookstore.) Provide simple rhythm instruments, such as drums, sand blocks, or a xylophone, as well as the instruments from "Jungle-Jammin' Instruments" on page 56.

Furry Feet Dance To The Beat

Bring out those funny, furry feet you created from fuzzy slippers (see "Furry Feet" page 56) and your preschoolers will be transformed into dancing creatures of the jungle!

Tactile experience
Weight discrimination
Gross-motor skills
Measurement skills
Socialization

Quicksand!

For an ooey-gooey, *almost* true-to-life quicksand experience, pour four to six boxes of cornstarch into a tub, sensory table, or plastic pool. Add enough water to make it drippy, but not too runny. Add food coloring (green looks great!), some putty knives, and some wooden spoons for stirring. If the mixture dries overnight, simply add more water. This recipe will last for about a week. It's messy—but it washes right off!

The Swamplands

Add a few bags of green Easter grass to a sensory table; then fill it with water. Add pasta forks, tongs, or rubber spatulas for stirring. After a few days, surprise your students with some wriggly rubber fishing worms hiding at the bottom! (To reuse the grass: drain it, let it dry, and store it in a box.)

Jungle Puddles

Where does all that rain in the rain forest go, anyway? Into puddles, of course! Create the intriguing look of jungle puddles by tinting a pool of water with a few drops of blue and green food coloring. Add shimmer with a handful of sequins. Provide youngsters with a couple of aquarium nets so they can "catch" the sparkle and shine!

Science Center

Fine-motor skills
Gross-motor skills
Analytical thinking
Observation skills

Hey, There's A Jungle In Here!

You don't have to have a green thumb to plant your own rain forest! All you need is a pool full of potting soil and some 100% guaranteed-to-grow birdseed. Have children sprinkle and stir birdseed into the soil for a few days. On a Friday, add water until the soil is thoroughly moistened. Cover the pool lightly with a sheet of plastic. On Monday you should see the beginnings of your very own birdseed jungle! Be sure to have a few magnifying glasses nearby for curious explorers.

Scents Of The Rain Forest

Get out the pineapple, coconut, vanilla, and banana extracts. Pour a few drops of each one onto a cotton ball; then place each cotton ball in a salt shaker or a bowl for children to smell. Can they guess which fruit is represented by each scent? Encourage connections by placing some real fruit on the table, as well as boxes or pictures of products made from tropical fruit.

In The Jungle

We went for a walk in the jungle. The trees were really tall. Monkeys were way up high. They were swinging by their tails. Amy saw a big snake. It was purple! A parrot talked to Jason. It said "Why are you in my jungle?"

On A Jungle Walk

After planting a birdseed jungle (see "Hey, There's A Jungle In Here!" on page 62), ask youngsters to imagine what it might feel like to be a tiny ant crawling around in there. Would the plants seem enormous? That's how it would feel for us if we were in a jungle! Write a class story about what the children might see or do if they found themselves walking around in the rain forest. Hang up the completed story for all to see.

Snaky Stories

Cut a supply of bulletin-board paper to resemble long, curly snakes. Encourage children to use their imaginations as they dictate and illustrate their own original jungle stories onto these snaky shapes. Invite your writers to share their stories with the class.

Kelly saw a tiger in the jungle.

Happy Habitat

Go wild in the block area! Bring in stuffed jungle animal toys (or laminate pictures of some); then strategically tuck them into the shelves and corners of your block area. Add some binoculars (fashioned from pairs of toilet-tissue tubes) and a broken camera (or a toy one). A few bamboo branches or a large tropical houseplant will enhance your jungle, too. Invite little ones to grab their backpacks and head into the wilds of this jungle habitat.

Tips For An Extended Stay

You've got quicksand and jungle critters and tropical foods in your centers. Now try these group, outdoor, and parent-involvement ideas to extend your jungle theme.

Which jungle fruit do you like the best?					
banana	Tess	Rob	Kellie	Jonas	Kyla
pineapple	Martin	Piel			
coconut	Shanna	Terese	Malik		
mango	Faiza				
star fruit	Cher	Katie			

All Together Now

Take the fruits from your dramatic-play center (see "Fruits Of The Tropics" on page 60), add a few bananas, and have a tropical-fruit-tasting party! Peel and slice the various fruits to provide each child with a taste of each one. Then graph the results. Which jungle goodie is your class's favorite?

Out 'n' About

How can you bring a little piece of the jungle to your school or center grounds? Have your children plant a tree! They'll love digging the hole, feeling the dirt, and watching the seedling go into the ground. Who knows? They may return with their own children in years to come to visit *their* tree!

Family Focus

Invite parents to come and join the jungle fun in your classroom. They can try their hands in the art area, do a little jungle jammin', and explore the quicksand and the swamplands. Have your little ones help prepare some delicious tropical fruit salad as a refreshing snack.

Highlights Of Our Trip
Adventure In The Jungle

Our jungle expedition took us through quicksand, past snakes and other creepy-crawly critters, and deep into the rain forest. Take a look!

Ten, nine, eight…Better buckle up 'cause you're in for a trip that's out of this world! Rocket ships, shooting stars, and UFOs are all a part of this classroom journey to outer space.

Off To Outer Space

ADMIT ONE

Getting Ready To Go!

Load up the space capsule with the supplies you'll need to create the centers of your choice (see the lists on page 67). Then check out the preparation ideas on this page to make your space journey *really* special! Ready? Let's blast off!

ADMIT ONE

Planets Overhead

You can turn your classroom ceiling into an instant planetarium by carefully cutting out planets from colored foam core (found in office supply and craft stores). Decorate the cutouts with fabric paints or paint markers; then dust them with glitter. Punch holes in the tops of the planets and suspend them from the ceiling with heavy nylon thread. These will last for years if stored with care.

3-2-1…Blast Off!

What do a refrigerator box and a rocket ship have in common? The captive imaginations of preschoolers! Cut out a big, back door for easy entry and an oval window (at eye level) in the front of the ship. Hot-glue milk jug lids and various plastic container tops on the inside of the box to make your rocket ship's control panel.

Don't Forget Your Oxygen!

Wondering what *else* you could do with those oatmeal containers? Turn them into oxygen tanks for your wandering astronauts. Just cover an oatmeal canister with aluminum foil. Then make two slits in opposite sides of the canister and pull a length of thick elastic through the slits. Tie the elastic into a belt-sized loop. A child wears this by stepping into the elastic loop and pulling it up around her waist.

Space Stuff

Choose from the center ideas on pages 68–73. Here's a handy list of the supplies you'll need to prepare each one.

Art Area

Space Pictures: black construction paper, neon poster board, scissors, glue, gummed stars

Paint, Press, And Peel: bubble wrap, small paint rollers, silver and/or yellow paint, black construction paper

Imaginative UFOs: Styrofoam® plates and bowls, boundary tape or crepe-paper streamers, collage materials, "plue"

Space Chalk: black construction paper or black roofing paper, sugar chalk

Dramatic-Play Center

In An Astronaut's Kitchen: oven mitts, rubber boots, aluminum foil, aluminum pie plates, Styrofoam® packing peanuts

Reading Center

Space Station For Imagination: large cardboard boxes, scissors, white paint, paintbrushes, aluminum foil, glue, flashlights, space-related books and magazines

Music And Movement

Lighter Than Air: laminated poster-board stars, mittens, rubber boots, oxygen tanks (see page 66), slow instrumental music

Slow Motion: record album and player

Science Center

Galaxy In A Bottle: plastic soft-drink bottles, marbles, star-shaped foil confetti, hot glue, magnifying glasses, flashlights

Constellation Creations: large appliance box, black paper, scissors, glow-in-the-dark stars, flashlight

Writing Center

I'm Going On The Space Shuttle, And I'm Taking…: chart paper, markers, crayons

Rocket Into Writing: white paper cut into rocket shapes, crayons

Sensory Tables And Tubs

Moon Putty: liquid starch, white glue, blue and silver glitter

Stirring Up A Galaxy: blue food coloring, foil confetti, tinsel or foil Christmas-tree garland

Bobbing In Space: Ping-Pong® balls, muffin tins, slotted spoons, strainers, plastic tongs

Whoa! Landing On Earth!: golf balls, dish detergent, muffin tins, slotted spoons, strainers, plastic tongs

Block Area

Intergalactic Constructions: blocks of Styrofoam® packaging

Art Area

Fine-motor skills
Hand-eye coordination
Color and shape recognition
Cognitive skills

Space Pictures

Invite children to use black construction paper as the dark space background for a creative look at space! Provide neon poster board for youngsters to cut into planet shapes and gummed stars for children to stick onto their papers. They'll create a whole universe in no time!

Paint, Press, And Peel

Instead of paper, clip a large sheet of bubble wrap onto your easel. Then encourage a child to use small rollers to paint with silver or yellow tempera paint. To make a monoprint of the masterpiece, just press a sheet of black construction paper on the bubble wrap, rub gently, and then peel it off.

Space Chalk

Make some sugar chalk (see page 5), and invite your preschoolers to draw space pictures on black paper. To make a class mural, have youngsters draw their designs on black roofing paper (found at hardware stores). It's extra sturdy and goes for miles!

Imaginative UFOs

How do you make a UFO? Any way you want to! Provide a combination of Styrofoam® plates and bowls, rolls of boundary tape (found at hardware stores) or crepe-paper streamers, plastic beads, pipe cleaners, foil scraps, and anything else you can think of. Invite a young artist to put it all together with some colored "plue" (see page 4). Take the finished UFOs out on the playground when they're dry to see if they'll fly!

Space Station For Imagination

It just takes a bit of preparation to transform your reading area into an intergalactic space station where your young astronauts can come to explore the final frontier—their imaginations! Gather a few large cardboard boxes. Cut doors into each box; then ask your young ground crew to help you decorate the boxes with white paint and pieces of aluminum foil. Provide some flashlights and an assortment of space-related books and magazines. Invite young space enthusiasts to crawl inside the space station to look at books in the deep dark of space!

Zoom! Zoom! Zoom! I'm Off To The Moon!

By Dan Yaccarino

Scholastic Trade Books

Blast Off!: Poems About Space

Edited by Lee Bennett Hopkins

HarperCollins Children's Books

Books In Space

Blast into storytime with some of these space-book selections. Be sure to shuttle these books over to your reading area for children to enjoy on their own when story-time's through.

Me And My Place In Space

By Joan Sweeney

Crown Publishers, Inc.

I Want To Be An Astronaut

By Byron Barton

HarperCollins Juvenile Books

Big Silver Space Shuttle

By Ken Wilson-Max

Cartwheel Books

Dramatic-Play Center

Creative thinking
Motor skills
Socialization

In An Astronaut's Kitchen

It's not easy to maneuver in the kitchen when you're wearing astronaut gear! Provide big oven mitts and rubber boots for children to wear in your home living area. Cover your table with aluminum foil and have youngsters serve space meals on aluminum pie plates. For a meal that's lighter than air, they can stir up a pot of Styrofoam® packing peanuts—green or white!

Music And Movement

Auditory skills
Gross-motor skills
Creative thinking
Socialization

Lighter Than Air

Cut some stars from poster board; then laminate them and scatter them on the floor. Provide adult-sized mittens and rubber boots, as well as the oxygen tanks made in "Don't Forget Your Oxygen!" (page 66). Put on some slow instrumental music and invite your children to prance through space!

Slow Motion

For a change of pace, play an album (any album) on the slowest speed of your record player. Encourage children to move to this s-l-o-w sound. Just have them pretend their feet are stuck in gooey moon gum!

Moon Putty

Could this be what the moon really feels like? If so, let's go! Combine two or three bottles of liquid starch with one gallon of white glue and lots of blue and silver glitter. Knead the mixture until it becomes a nonsticky, but very pliable, putty. Plop the whole mass into an empty water table or tub. (Position this station away from any water source or you'll end up with Moon Goo.) Your space scientists will want to revisit this station again and again! Store the putty in the fridge, lightly covered. It can keep for about a month; just add small amounts of starch to prevent it from getting sticky. Note: If Moon Putty should get on clothes or carpet, simply soak overnight in water.

Fine-motor skills
Gross-motor skills
Tactile discrimination
Measurement skills
Socialization

Stirring Up A Galaxy

Fill a tub or water table with water tinted dark blue. Then sprinkle in a couple of handfuls of foil confetti. Float tinsel or pieces of Christmas-tree garland on top of the water for an extraspecial galactic effect!

Bobbing In Space

Transform Ping-Pong® balls into weightless moon rocks when you add them to your water table. Add muffin tins, slotted spoons, small strainers, or even plastic tongs to provide a challenging mission for little hands.

Whoa! Landing On Earth!

What is weightless in space is heavy on Earth! Demonstrate this by having yet another tub or pool filled with *heavy* moon rocks—golf balls! This time add just a small amount of water and lots of dish detergent to make the balls slippery. Have the same tools available as you do for the center described in "Bobbing In Space" so children can compare the difference between the two stations.

Writing Center

Creative language and thought processing
Word association
Writing
Socialization

I'm Going On The Space Shuttle, And I'm Taking...

What would you take on a trip to outer space? A flashlight? A box of doughnuts? Your pet monkey? Your team of astronauts will have all kinds of interesting things to list. Invite students to dictate their "must-haves" for you to write on a sheet of chart paper; then have them add illustrations. Display the list in your room, and review it periodically throughout your unit.

Rocket Into Writing

Spark thoughts about space travel by providing each author with a sheet of white construction paper cut into the shape of a rocket. This tip is sure to ignite some super space stories!

What should we take on the space shuttle?

Justin – a camera

Monique – my teddy bear

Ruth – bananas

Phillip – astronaut food

Kyle – my dad

Block Area

Gross-motor skills
Problem solving
Weight and size discrimination
Socialization

Intergalactic Constructions

Collect blocks of Styrofoam® packaging in different sizes and shapes (the kind found in appliance boxes). Add these to your everyday blocks. They'll launch creative constructions that will send your kids to the moon and back!

Galaxy In A Bottle

Fill plastic soft-drink bottles with water and different colors of marbles. Add a sprinkle of star-shaped foil confetti to each bottle before securing the bottle top with a squirt of hot glue. Encourage youngsters to roll these on the floor, or simply shake them and observe the movement of the objects inside. Put some magnifying glasses and flashlights nearby for the investigators in your room.

Constellation Creations

Line the inside of a large appliance box with black paper; then stick on glow-in-the-dark stars (available in toy stores). Cut a flap door in the box. Invite your young astronomers to sit inside the box with a flashlight and "connect" the stars with lines of light.

After decking out your centers for a space visit, try these ideas for a group project, outdoor fun, and parent involvement.

Tips For An Extended Stay

All Together Now

You really *can* have the moon…or at least, you can make it! Begin with a *big* plastic ball as a form. Have children use diluted white glue to adhere layers of white tissue-paper pieces to the ball. Keep this project going for several days, so you have *lots* of layers. A sprinkling of glittery "stardust" at the end will give your moon a special glow. Find a spot on the ceiling and hang it up. OK…ready to make the sun?

Family Focus

Your space aces will be anxious to give their parents a tour of all the fun centers in your cosmic classroom. Invite parents to join you for an afternoon of space exploration and a snack—moon pies, of course!

Out 'n' About

Send your explorers on a hunt for moon rocks! For older children, use shiny stones available in the floral section of your local discount store. For preschoolers under four, stick to Ping-Pong® balls. Hide the "moon rocks" around your playground area. Invite your students to find the rocks, then hide them again for their fellow astronauts to find.

Highlights Of Our Trip
Off To Outer Space

Four, three, two, one…blast off! From launching UFOs to chasing shooting stars, we've had a trip that was out of this world! Here's a peek at all the fun we had.

75

Goin' To The Farm

If your little ones find farm life intriguing, then they'll flock to your classroom barnyard! So bring out the birdseed, the beans, and the biscuits…we're goin' to the farm!

Getting Ready To Go!

Load up the wagon with the supplies you'll need to create your choice of centers for this farmyard frolic. Check out the handy lists on page 77 to help you get organized. Then invite youngsters to help you with a few extra chores that will really make your farm theme something to crow about!

ADMIT ONE

ADMIT ONE

Farm Fences

Purchase some plastic lattice at your local hardware store. It's relatively inexpensive and very durable. To hold a piece of lattice upright, slip the legs of a child's chair through the holes at each end. Use the lattice pieces to mark off stations and to add an outside flair to your inside farm!

Here A Cow, There A Cow...

Invite children to bring in stuffed animals from home to add a more authentic feel to your block-area barnyard (see page 82).

How About A Little Music?

Visit your local library to find recordings of folk or bluegrass music. Pick a few to play in your classroom to enhance the farm atmosphere.

Fixin' Up The Farm

Choose from the center ideas on pages 78–83. Here's a handy list of the supplies you'll need to prepare each one.

Art Area

Barnyard In A Box: shoeboxes, construction paper, scissors, glue, craft sticks, potting soil, straw, popcorn kernels, birdseed, felt, pom-poms, tacky glue

Corn-On-The-Cob Prints: corn on the cob, paint, large sheets of paper

With A Quack, Quack Here…: pair of child's swim flippers; paint; large, shallow pan; long length of bulletin-board paper

Dramatic-Play Center

A Country Kitchen: small iron skillet, plastic eggs, rolling pins, biscuit cutters, white play dough, red and white checkered tablecloth

Reading Center

Hay, Hay, Hay—Let's Read!: bales of hay, wheelbarrow or wagon, stuffed farm animals, pairs of children's denim overalls

Sensory Tables And Tubs

Chicks 'n' Eggs: yellow pom-poms, plastic eggs, green Easter grass

Pigs In The Mud: pink balloons; permanent marker; real mud, chocolate pudding, or dish detergent colored with red and green food coloring

Just Scratchin' The Surface: pasta forks, popcorn, birdseed

Block Area

In The Farmyard: plastic lattice, children's overalls, work gloves, toy garden tools, wheelbarrow or wagon, stuffed farm animals

Science Center

How Does Your Garden Grow?: bean seeds, grass seeds, flower seeds, plastic bags, small flowerpots, soil, magnifying glasses, paper, crayons

Who Has It? Who Doesn't?: farm-animal pictures, sentence strips, craft feather, craft fur, baskets

Writing Center

Old MacDonald Had A…: chart paper, markers, cassette player and tape (optional)

What If You Were A Farmer?: barn-shaped sheets of paper, crayons

Music And Movement

Grab A Partner: musical recordings, rhythm instruments

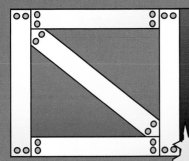
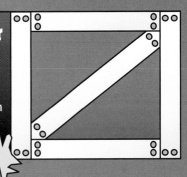

Fine-motor skills
Hand-eye coordination
Cognitive skills
Visual expression
Sequencing

Barnyard In A Box

Invite your young artists to create their very own itty-bitty barnyards! To make a barnyard in a box, glue a construction-paper sky, barn, and trees to the inside bottom of a shoebox. Add a fence made from craft sticks; then let the glue dry overnight. Turn the box on its side and make the yard by gluing down real potting soil, pieces of straw, popcorn kernels, and birdseed. Now you're ready to bring in some barnyard friends. Simply use tacky glue to attach felt eyes, beaks, noses, and mouths onto large pom-poms. Keep this activity out all week. Children will surprise you with the creative ways they construct their farms!

Corn-On-The-Cob Prints

Use dried corn on the cob for this playful way to print. Have a child roll a cob in tempera paint, then roll it on a large sheet of paper. Encourage children to squirt different colors of paint onto their papers, then roll the cobs through the paint to see how the colors blend. Yes, it's messy—but it's fun!

With A Quack, Quack Here...

What would it be like to walk like a duck? Your wee friends will find out with this unusual painting project! Have a child slip into a pair of rubber flippers and make "duck prints" by stepping into a shallow pan of tempera paint and then onto a length of bulletin-board paper. Each artist can waddle solo or invite the whole flock to participate for a giant work of art that's just ducky!

Vocabulary development
Attention span
Receptive and expressive language skills

Hay, Hay, Hay—Let's Read!

There's nothing like a few bales of hay to really lend that farm feeling to your reading center. (Check to be sure no one in your room is allergic to hay before bringing it in.) Borrow a wheelbarrow or a red wagon for holding farm-themed books. Then add some farm life—the sweet-smelling, cuddly kind, of course! Also put a couple of pairs of denim overalls at this center. Your readers can suit up, pick a book, and hop on a hay bale for a good read!

First-Rate Farm Books

Rise 'n' shine for storytime! There's no shortage of great children's books about the farm. Here are just a few.

Barnyard Banter
By Denise Fleming
Henry Holt And Company, Inc.

Farmer Nat: A Lift-The-Flap Book
By Chris Demarest
Red Wagon Books

Picnic Farm
By Christine Morton
Holiday House, Inc.

Cows In The Kitchen
By June Crebbin
Candlewick Press

Big Red Barn
By Margaret Wise Brown
HarperCollins Children's Books

Cock-A-Doodle-Doo: A Farmyard Counting Book
By Steve Lavis
Lodestar Books

Dramatic-Play Center

Creative thinking
Verbal skills
Socialization

A Country Kitchen

Fill your home-living center with the comforts of a country kitchen! Get out the old iron skillet, farm-fresh eggs (colored plastic ones will do), rolling pins, and biscuit cutters. Plain white play dough makes *fabulous* biscuits! For a final touch, set your table with a red and white checkered cloth.

Music And Movement

Auditory skills
Sound and rhythm discrimination
Socialization

Grab A Partner

Bring out the recordings you gathered for "How About A Little Music?" (page 76), as well as any children's recordings with farm-related songs—such as Raffi's version of "Down On Grandpa's Farm" (from *One Light One Sun,* Troubadour Records Ltd.) or "Down On The Farm" by Greg and Steve (from *We All Live Together, Volume 5,* Youngheart Music, Inc.). Provide some rhythm instruments and plenty of room to square-dance!

Fine-motor skills
Sensory discrimination
Sorting
Counting
Socialization

Pigs In The Mud

Pigs are messy but marvelous, and so is this station! Fill pink balloons with water; then turn them into baby pigs by adding eyes, ears, and a snout with a permanent marker. (The knot in the balloon makes the perfect piggy tail!) Place your pigs in a tub of mud. Or, for a cleaner alternative, fill the tub with dish detergent you've made to *look* like mud by adding red and green food coloring to it. (Chocolate pudding makes *really* great mud, too!)

Note: Provide supervision and promptly remove any popped balloons to prevent a choking hazard.

Chicks 'n' Eggs

Tuck yellow pom-pom "chicks" inside colored plastic eggs. Then hide these chicks-to-be in a pool full of green Easter grass. See how many chicks your farmers can find…and hide!

Just Scratchin' The Surface

It just wouldn't be a farm unless you fed the chickens! So get out your pasta forks (chicken feet, of course!) and fill a pool with a mixture of popcorn and birdseed. Your preschoolers will love this! When they tire of this station, have them use the birdseed to feed their fine-feathered friends.

Writing Center

Creative language and thought processing
Word association
Auditory skills
Socialization

What If You Were A Farmer?

What would it be like to live on a farm? What animals would you have and what work would you do? Have children consider these questions as they compose and illustrate their own stories on barn-shaped sheets of paper.

I would have lots of sheep. They are cute!

Old MacDonald Had A...

Polar bear? Snake? Goldfish? Take a bit of poetic license with this traditional song and ask children to think of animals they wouldn't normally see on a farm. Record the verses as they choose animals and sing. Just for fun, try recording your class version on a cassette player and add it to your music collection! Bet it tops the charts!

Block Area

Fine-motor skills
Gross-motor skills
Verbal skills
Creative thinking

In The Farmyard

Transform your block area into a farmyard by adding a piece of plastic lattice (see "Farm Fences" on page 76). Provide farm-related props, such as overalls, work gloves, toy garden tools, and a wheelbarrow or wagon. And just to make your farm *extra* lively, add a variety of stuffed animals that children have brought from home. Now, let's milk those cows and gather those eggs!

How Does Your Garden Grow?

Plant some knowledge about seed germination and growth in your science center. Place a few bean seeds, grass seeds, and flower seeds in separate zippered plastic bags. Add a bit of water to each bag. Plant some of the same seeds in small pots of soil and keep them moist. Place the bags and pots in your science area (preferably near a window). Provide magnifying glasses, paper, and crayons. Have youngsters observe the seeds and document their findings.

Who Has It? Who Doesn't?

Create a matching game to help children categorize farm animals according to their covering—fur or feathers. Gather some farm-animal pictures (from magazines, clip art, or your own drawings). Make two labels—one that says "feathers" and has a craft feather glued to it and another that says "fur" and has a small square of craft fur glued to it. Place the labels next to two baskets; then ask children at this center to sort the animal pictures.

feathers   fur

After filling your centers with the sights and sounds of the farm, try these ideas for group time, outdoor play, and parent involvement. They're sure to please your young farmhands!

All Together Now

Make a cooperative—and creative—barnyard mural. Have children work together to paint a long, sturdy sheet of cardboard light blue. Then have them glue a mixture of birdseed, popcorn kernels, dried beans, seeds, and potting soil across the bottom. Provide magazines and invite youngsters to hunt for pictures of animals to clip out and glue onto their mural. (You may be surprised at the animals on *this* farm!) Keep this activity out for a while so it can grow and grow.

Out 'n' About

Find a small plot of earth (or create one by filling a baby pool with soil), provide sand shovels, and let your little farmers dig to their hearts' content! When it's planting time, provide birdseed, grass seed, or flower and vegetable seedlings. Then invite your farmers to tend these crops each day during outdoor play.

Fresh Vegetables

Seeds

Family Focus

Invite parents to join you on a field trip to a local farm or orchard to see and perhaps pick the fresh fruit or veggies of the season. If there's no farm nearby, try visiting a farmer's market to see a wide array of fresh fruits and vegetables. Have each child buy something to eat at snacktime that day. Mmmm!

84

Highlights Of Our Trip
Goin' To The Farm
We've been diggin' in the garden and scratchin' in the chicken feed. Life in the barnyard was fun, fun, fun!

By The Sea

Beach sand, seashells, and squiggly underwater friends catch the imaginations of all young fishermen as they explore the watery deep. There's plenty of fun in the sun while children are immersed in a sensory-rich environment that's *almost* as fun as the real beach!

ADMIT ONE

Getting Ready To Go!

Get ready for a "sea-sational" adventure by gathering the supplies you need from the lists on page 87 (depending on your choice of centers). Then prepare some of these props to enhance your seagoing theme.

ADMIT ONE

Is It Hot In Here?

Give your classroom a "beach-y" feeling with beach towels, sunglasses, inner tubes, flippers, and goggles. A propped-up beach umbrella would be perfect hovering over your teacher's chair…

Roll In The Ocean

Several uncut yards of inexpensive blue polyester will resemble a rippling ocean in your group area. Add some authentic fishnets and real shells to get your little ones in the mood to "fish" for learning!

Turn On The Tunes

Visit your local library for recordings of calypso music to add a lively touch to your center times. For a quieter feel during rest time or transitions, pop in a tape of ocean sounds. (You can use this again for "Sounds Of The Sea" on page 90.)

Beach Gear

Choose from the center ideas on pages 88–93. Here's a handy list of the supplies you'll need to prepare each one.

Art Area

Jiggly Jellyfish Kites: sugar chalk, white paper plates, glue, strips of cellophane, hole puncher, yarn or chenille stems

The Shimmering, Shining Sea: aluminum foil; blue and green paint; paintbrushes; white, blue, or green construction paper

Now That's A Big Fish!: bulletin-board paper, marker, natural sponges, paint, scissors

Deep-Sea Collages: construction paper; clear Con-Tact® covering; blue, green, and yellow cellophane strips; scissors; brightly colored foil gift wrap; sequins

Reading Center

Underwater Reading: diving gear, beach towels, children's sunglasses, small inflatable boat

Music And Movement

Sounds Of The Sea: recording of ocean sounds, chenille stems, strips of blue and opalescent cellophane

Writing Center

"That Fish Was This Big…": chart paper, markers

Fish Stories: paper cut into shapes of fish, starfish, whales, or sharks; crayons

Sensory Tables And Tubs

"Fish-A-Ma-Bobbers": plastic bobbers (for fishing line); slotted spoons, ice-cream scoops, and/or wire strainers

Fishin' The Fun Way: balloons, dish detergent, something to cover floor around pool

Searching For Shells And Stones: playground or beach sand, shells or stones, sand pails, shovels

Shimmering Seaweed!: blue food coloring, green or opalescent shredded gift packaging, silver or clear plastic bowl, spoons or rubber spatulas

Science Center

Bottles From The Sea: 32-ounce plastic bottles with caps, small shells, Easter grass, small balloons, blue or opalescent cellophane strips, hot glue

Dramatic-Play Center

Fish Fry: cans of salmon and tuna; empty boxes of frozen fish, french fries, and vegetables; frying pans; spatulas; pot holders; paper plates; red or blue checkered tablecloth

Block Area

Gone Fishin': laundry baskets or boxes, tagboard fish, paper clips, magnetic fishing poles

How Big Is A Blue Whale?: masking tape, measuring tape, picture of blue whale

Art Area

Fine-motor skills
Hand-eye coordination
Cognitive skills
Color and shape recognition
Counting

Jiggly Jellyfish Kites

Have children make jellyfish bodies by coloring white paper plates with sugar chalk (see page 5). Then have them glue on cellophane-strip tentacles. Punch two holes at the top of each plate and attach a length of yarn or a chenille stem for a handle. These jellyfish jiggle like kites in the wind when they're dry.

Now *That's* A Big Fish!

On a long length of bulletin-board paper, draw the outline of a huge fish. Invite your young artists to paint it, using natural sponges to make prints with different colors of tempera. When the fish is complete and dry, cut it out. Then hang it in your "classroom aquarium" or in a hallway for all to see.

Deep-Sea Collages

Prepare this activity by cutting the centers from colorful sheets of construction paper to create frames. For each artist, lay a piece of clear Con-Tact® covering sticky side up on a table. Then stick a paper frame onto the Con-Tact® covering. Each child can make a water scene by sticking on blue, green, and yellow cellophane strips. Encourage him to tear or cut sea creatures from brightly colored foil gift wrap or construction paper. A splash of sequins will add sparkle to this sea!

The Shimmering, Shining Sea

For dreamy watercolors, cover your easel with aluminum foil and invite children to paint the foil with shades of blue and green. When a child is ready to take a piece of her ocean home, make a monoprint on white, blue, or green construction paper (see page 5). This process can be repeated several times, either by continuing to add paint to the design, or by wiping off the easel with a damp cloth and beginning again.

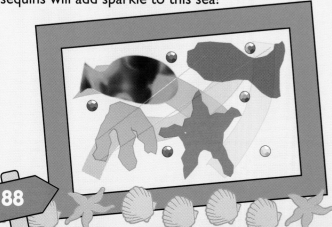

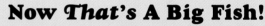

Underwater Reading

Set the mood for a story about the ocean by dressing as if you were headed there yourself. Beg a dive shop or a scuba-certified friend to let you borrow a few props, such as a diving vest, a pair of flippers, or goggles. Spread out beach towels for youngsters to relax on while you read. When storytime's over, add the towels and some cheap sunglasses to your reading area. Plus a small inflatable boat makes the perfect nook for any sailor's adventure into a great book!

Seaworthy Stories

There are a boatload of great books with an ocean or beach theme! Here are just a few.

A House For Hermit Crab
By Eric Carle
Simon & Schuster

At The Beach
By Anne Rockwell
Aladdin Paperbacks

A Beach Day
By Douglas Florian
Greenwillow Books

One Sun: A Book Of Terse Verse
By Bruce McMillan
Holiday House, Inc.

Across The Big Blue Sea: An Ocean Wildlife Book
By Jakki Wood
National Geographic Society

Dramatic-Play Center

Creative thinking
Verbal skills
Sequencing
Socialization

Fish Fry

Stock up on unopened cans of salmon and tuna and empty boxes of frozen fish fillets 'cause we're going to have a good old-fashioned Southern fish fry! Just gather those cans and empty packages of fish, french fries, and a few vegetables, of course! Supply a few frying pans, some spatulas, a couple of sets of pot holders, and a big supply of paper plates. A red or blue checkered tablecloth on the table will add the perfect finishing touch!

Music And Movement

Auditory discrimination
Gross-motor skills
Socialization

Sounds Of
The Sea

The sounds of the sea are available on recordings at the library or in bookstores; they're often accompanied by soothing classical music. Make some simple props for creative movement by twisting chenille stems around strips of blue and opalescent cellophane. Encourage youngsters to move like ocean creatures in the deep water or on the sandy beach.

Tactile discrimination
Analytical thinking
Fine-motor skills
Socialization

"Fish-A-Ma-Bobbers"

Fill a sensory table or pool with water; then drop in several sizes of brightly colored plastic bobbers used to float fishing lines. Throw in slotted spoons, ice-cream scoops, or small wire strainers for easy bobber handling!

Searching For Shells And Stones

You can't have a beach without sand and shells or stones, depending on which coast you're visiting. Pour a bag of clean white playground sand in a tub (or add real beach sand, if you're near the ocean). Ask parents to donate shells or collect some stones from your area. Tuck them in the sand for youngsters to discover. Add a few sand pails and shovels for this expedition!

Fishin' The Fun Way

Fill a dozen or more colorful balloons with water and put them in a shallow pool or tub on a covered area of the floor. Add enough dish detergent and a squirt of water to make a slippery, sudsy solution. Then invite your young fishermen to reach right in and fish with their hands! Watch out—these fish may jump right out of the pool!

Shimmering Seaweed!

Tint a pool of water with blue food coloring; then add a package or two of green or opalescent shredded gift packaging. Float a silver or clear plastic bowl on top, and add spoons or rubber spatulas for stirring.

Writing Center

Creative language and thought processing
Word association
Writing
Socialization

Fish Stories

Cut out pages in the shape of fish and see what kinds of fish stories your youngsters come up with! For variety, cut paper into the shape of starfish or whales or sharks and you'll soon have an ocean full of sea-creature stories!

Corina

My grandpa likes to fish at the beach.

"That Fish Was This Big..."

Introduce your little ones to exaggeration when you string along a whale of a tale. Start a story by saying, "One day we were on the beach and [Jeremy] saw…" Have the child named finish the sentence. Then add a sentence about another child and have her add an outlandish event to the tale. Continue until you have a wild and wonderful class story!

Science Center

Visual discrimination
Analytical thinking

Bottles From The Sea

For a hands-on study of light refraction, make these interesting ocean bottles. Into each of several 32-ounce plastic bottles put shells, Easter grass "seaweed," water balloon "fish," or blue and opalescent cellophane strips. Then fill each bottle to the brim with water before sealing the cap in place with hot glue. Ask youngsters to look carefully at the items in each bottle. Do the objects change size in the water? What happens when the light shines through?

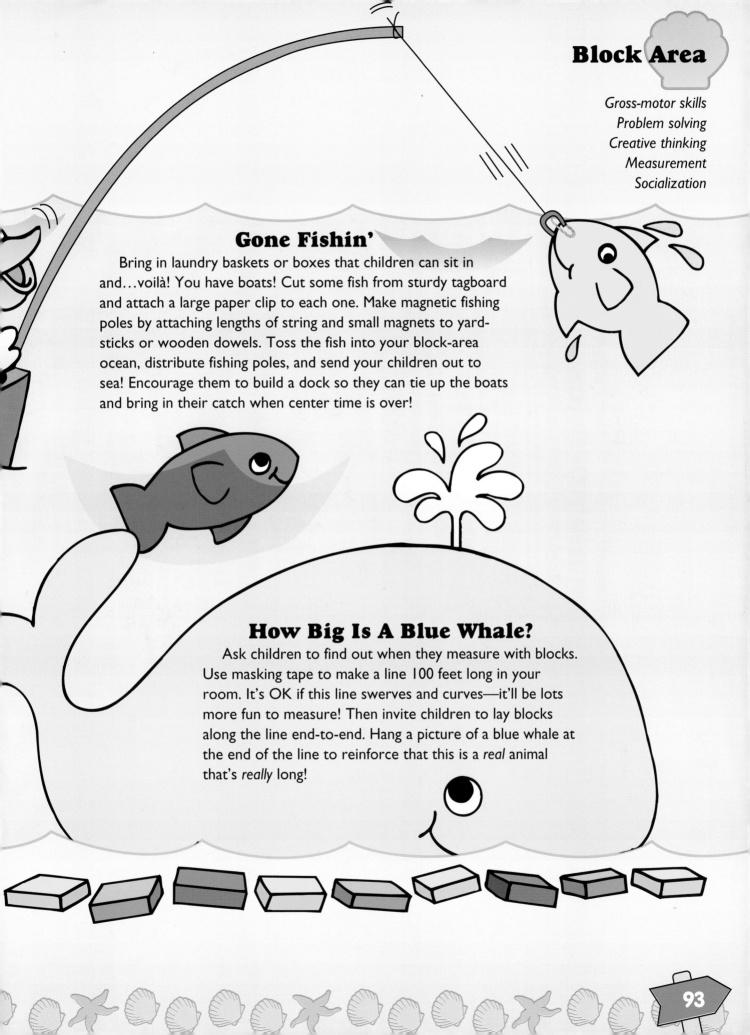

Block Area

Gross-motor skills
Problem solving
Creative thinking
Measurement
Socialization

Gone Fishin'

Bring in laundry baskets or boxes that children can sit in and…voilà! You have boats! Cut some fish from sturdy tagboard and attach a large paper clip to each one. Make magnetic fishing poles by attaching lengths of string and small magnets to yardsticks or wooden dowels. Toss the fish into your block-area ocean, distribute fishing poles, and send your children out to sea! Encourage them to build a dock so they can tie up the boats and bring in their catch when center time is over!

How Big Is A Blue Whale?

Ask children to find out when they measure with blocks. Use masking tape to make a line 100 feet long in your room. It's OK if this line swerves and curves—it'll be lots more fun to measure! Then invite children to lay blocks along the line end-to-end. Hang a picture of a blue whale at the end of the line to reinforce that this is a *real* animal that's *really* long!

Tips For An Extended Stay

Your centers are decked out with fishing poles, seaweed, and sharks. Now try these ideas for a collaborative project, outdoor play, and parent involvement.

All Together Now

Encourage all your little ones to collect seashells from home to contribute to this group art project. In advance, coat the inside of a disposable aluminum pan with petroleum jelly. Place a piece of looped wire or yarn in the tray, with part of the loop hanging over the rim. This will serve as a hanger when the project is finished. Then prepare enough plaster of paris to partially fill the tray following the package directions. Pour the wet plaster into the tray. When it begins to set, have each child press a shell or two into the plaster. Top off the shell design with sprinkles of blue or iridescent glitter. Let the plaster harden completely (at least overnight). Then remove the project from the tray and hang it where everyone can enjoy it.

Out 'n' About

Grab a beach towel and slip into your swimsuit 'cause you're in for a day at the beach—no matter where you live! With a sunny day, a few seashells in the sandbox, the gentle spray of a sprinkler, and the vivid imaginations of your preschoolers, you'll find yourself enjoying the coast all day long! Make sure to have bubbles, beach balls, and other beach toys on hand. And don't forget your shades!

Family Focus

Invite parents to bring in some photos or home videos of family vacations at the beach. Children love to see other families in action. Moms, dads, and kids can tell about their family's favorite adventures at the beach or on the sea.

Highlights Of Our Trip
By The Sea

Have a seat and let us tell you about our trip to the beach and the super-duper, bigger-than-ever fish we caught! It's a whale of a tale!

Plan Your Own Classroom Adventure!

Destination: _____

Art Area

Reading Center

Dramatic-Play Center

Science Center

Sensory Tables And Tubs

Block Area

Writing Center

Music And Movement

Tips For An Extended Stay:

FUN—2 mi.